MAOIST INSURGENCY AND INDIA'S INTERNAL SECURITY ARCHITECTURE

MAOIST INSURGENCY AND INDIA'S INTERNAL SECURITY ARCHITECTURE

Edited by

EN Rammohan
Amrit Pal Singh
AK Agarwal

(Established 1870)

United Service Institution of India
New Delhi

Vij Books India Pvt Ltd
New Delhi, India

Published by

Vij Books India Pvt Ltd
(Publishers, Distributors & Importers)
2/19, Ansari Road, Darya Ganj
New Delhi - 110002
Phones: 91-11-43596460, 91-11- 65449971
Fax: 91-11-47340674
e-mail : vijbooks@rediffmail.com
web: www.vijbooks.com

Copyright © United Service Institution of India, New Delhi

ISBN: 978-93-81411-27-8

Contents

List of Abbreviations

ARC	Aviation Research Centre
ATUs	Anti TerroristUnits
BSF	Border Security Force
CBI	Central Bureau of Investigation
CBP	Customs and Border Protection
CCTNS	Crime and Criminal Tracking Network
CINT	Chief Intelligence Officer
CRPF	Central Reserve Police Force
CTC	Counter Terrorism Centre
DCI	Director of Central Intelligence
DHS	Department of Homeland Security
DIA	Defence Intelligence Agency
DNI	Director of National Intelligence
DOD	Department of Defence
DOJ	Department of Justice
FEMA	Federal Emergency Management Agency
FIGs	Field Intelligence Groups
HM	Home Minister
HSDN	Homeland Security Data Network
HUM INT	Human Intelligence

I&A	Office of Intelligence and Analysis
IC	Intelligence Community
ICE	Immigration and Custom Enforcement
IE	Intelligence Enterprise
ILO	Infrastructure Liaison Officer
ILP	International Liaison Programme
IPS	Indian Police Service
IRTPA	Intelligence Reform and Terrorism Prevention Act
IS	Internal Security
ISC	Information Sharing Council
ISE	Information Sharing Environment
ISR	Intelligence Surveillance and Reconnaissance
JIC	Joint Intelligence Committee
JTTF	Joint Terrorism Task Force
LATEW	Los Angeles Terrorism Early Warning
MACs	Multi-Agency Centres
MMP	Mission Mode Project
NCRB	National Crime Records Bureau
NCTC	National Counter Terrorism Centre
NIA	National Investigation Agency
NSA	National Security Agency/Advisor
NSG	National Security Guard
NTRO	National Technical Research Organisation

NYPD	New York Police Department.
PATRIOT	Providing Appropriate Tools Required to Intercept and ObstructTerrorism
PCLOB	Privacy and Civil Liberties Oversight Board
POTA	Prevention of Terrorism Act
PWG	Peoples War Group
QRTs	Quick Response Teams
RAAW	Research and Analysis Wing
SAR	Suspicious Activity Reporting
SMACs	Subsidiary Multi-Agency Centres
SOPs	Standard Operating Procedures
SPG	Special Protection Group
TADA	Terrorist and Disruptive Activities
TLOG	Terrorism Liaison Officer Group.
TSA	Transportation Security Administration
TTIC	Terrorism Threat Integration Centre
UAPA	Unlawful Activities Prevention Act
UAV	Unmanned Air Vehicle
US	United States
USCG	USCoast Guard
USCIS	USCitizenship and Immigration Services

Introduction

In all there are five chapters in this compilation which are inter-related. The first chapter deals with the Maoist insurgency in India and analyses the reasons that led to the Communist Party of India (CPI) taking up the cause of the lower castes and scheduled tribes being denied rights of ownership of cultivable land and forest land. There are two main issues that were debated by the Constituent Assembly. This led to inclusion of two Schedules —Fifth and Ninth in the Indian Constitution, in 1950.

The Fifth Schedule states that all Scheduled Areas, and Reserved Forests in mainland India are to be administered by a Tribal Advisory Council consisting of tribals living in that Scheduled Area. The Tribal Advisory Council was to be formed by the Governor of each State. The Governor was to report to the President of India on this. Regrettably, no Governor has exercised this right. The Governments of the States have acted illegally and unlawfully denying rights guaranteed to the Tribals in the Scheduled Areas. Some areas have even been leased to mining companies and tribals evicted from there.

The second issue pertains to ownership and equitable distribution of cultivable land. In Hindu society, ownership of cultivable land has been restricted to three upper castes. The CPI has been fighting for the lower castes to get them ownership rights of cultivable land. As per the Ninth Schedule of the Constitution, States were to legislate Land Ceiling laws so that people could get equitable share of cultivable land. All States passed such laws by 1955, but only three States - Jammu and Kashmir, West Bengal and Kerala implemented the Land Ceiling laws.

The CPI Maoists have been struggling in several states to see that land ceiling laws are enforced and forests administered by Tribal Advisory Councils. There is an ongoing fight with the Governments of Andhra Pradesh,

Maharashtra, Chattisgarh and Odisha where the Governments have leased forest land to mining companies without forming Tribal Advisory Councils. State Governments should follow the Constitution and the laws of the land to resolve the issue.

The Maoists have taken up arms. Their focus is on tribals and lower caste people for support. Stress is on militarisation with hierarchy and building of 'People's Guerrilla Army' capable of destroying the state machinery. Maoists have been targeting the government's buildings and infrastructure like jails, police stations, railway stations, blowing up buses, railway tracks and soon. Violence and breakdown of law and order is causing loss of innocent lives and damage to property. Maoists do not allow

construction of roads and undertaking of developmental activities essential for progress and removal of poverty in their areas. The Maoists have developed strategy to keep the government and its forces cleverly disorganised by employing tactical tools like abduction and hostages and forcing the government to concede their demands. They also make large sums of money through extortion and ransom.Following the Constitution; laws of the land; ensuring security and developmental work are intertwined, and need simultaneous resolution to settle this vexed problem.

The second chapter deals with use of air power in combating the Maoist insurgency. The author has suggested deployment of drones to detect insurgent camps in the forests and use of helicopters for evacuation of casualties and other measures to facilitate logistics support for Countering Insurgency.

An appraisal of India's Intelligence agencies has been covered in Chapter Three. Regrettably they are more aligned to the party in power than to the country. The Intelligence and Investigating agencies should shed this cozy association with the political parties and become truly professional in their approach.The fourth and fifth chapters are concerning the manner in which the United States has reacted after the 9/11 terrorist attack in the USA and how India reacted after the terrorist attack by the Lashkar-e Toiba in Mumbai on 26 November 2008. The papers focus on the way the United States has gone about tackling the issue effectively; and the rather dismal performance by India as a reaction to a similar terror attack.

There is a need to evolve a Comprehensive Internal Security Policy covering all dimensions and all levels-- political, economic and social. These are all interlinked. At times the required measures will conflict with each other. Going too far in one direction could be counter productive. Striking the right balance is the key to meeting the Internal Security challenges effectively.

1
The Maoist Insurgency

E N Rammohan

Introduction

The Naxalite insurgency in India captured the limelight when a revolt broke out in a sleepy village of North Bengal called Naxalbari in 1968. Earlier, in 1968, there was a similar rebellion, but on a much larger scale and for a longer duration, in Srikakulam district of Andhra Pradesh in what is called the Agency area of that district. Both these rebellions concerned the scheduled castes and scheduled tribes of these two areas rebelling against the Revenue administration and the State Government and taking the law into their own hands. To understand these two rebellions and the subsequent evolution of the Communist Party of India (CPI) to the CPI M then into the CPI ML and further into the CPI Maoist, one has to go back in history and understand what has happened in this country about the ownership of cultivable land and the rights of the Adivasis or forest dwellers on the forests in which they dwell.

The root causes of this problem can be summed up in one word-caste. This was the social system structured during the course of evolution of Hindu civilization. Four main castes were stratified in Hindu society. The first was the Brahmin who conducted the religious rituals on behalf of all the people of Hindu society. It was the *Brahmin* who interceded with the Gods on behalf of all the Hindu people. The second caste in hierarchical order was the *Kshatriya*, who constituted the soldiers who fought the enemies of the Hindus and who also policed their society. The third was the *Vaisya*, or *bania* who was the trader, who conducted the business of procuring merchandise and selling it to the three other castes. Last was the *shudra* who did various services for the three upper castes.

Below this were the untouchables or *harijans*, who performed even more degrading work like sanitation, washing clothes, handling waste of the three upper castes. Below this was another group, all Dravidians, who were the original inhabitants of the Indian Sub-continent when the Aryans began their slow colonization of our country. During this process of slow migration and occupation of the fertile valleys of the country the original inhabitants; the Dravidians were pushed away from the fertile valleys into the forests of the country. Devoid of the chance to take up cultivation, these Dravidian people became hunter gatherers and due to their sojourn in the forests came to be known as *Adivasis* or *Vanvasis* literally meaning forest dwellers. In classification, the *Brahmins, Kshatriyas* and the *Banias* or *Vaisyas* were considered as upper classes. The *Shudras* became other backward classes and the lower caste of cleaners and other menial trades became scheduled castes. The original inhabitants before the Aryans migrated to this subcontinent and who were pushed into the forests became the scheduled tribes.

The three upper castes also saw to it that the ownership of cultivable land was retained with them. The British, when they took over the country in 1857 from the East India Company, did not consider the lop sided ownership of cultivable land by the upper castes. They did make some effort in some states. For example in the Agency areas of Andhra in Srikakulam districts, the land at the foot hills of the Eastern Ghats was reserved for the scheduled castes and tribes by the British administration, but regrettably this was observed more in the breach then as per the law.

It was only after independence and the notification of the Constitution of India in 1950, that laws were legislated for controlling the ownership of acreage of cultivable land by its citizens. Article 31A and the Ninth Schedule of the Constitution lays down the provisions for land ceiling. Regrettably despite this strong legislation made in 1949 and 1950, the landlord lobbies managed to subvert the articles of the Constitution and the laws legislated under the provisions of the ninth Schedule. In some of the countries in the Asian region, the extent of land distributed upto 1970 was 43 percent of agricultural land in China, 32 percent in South Korea and 32 percent in Japan, whereas in India it resulted in redistribution of only 1.25 percent of the operational area. China upto 1980 had distributed 90 percent of her agricultural land.[1]

In India landed property is the most important property, because India lives in its villages. Article 39 (b) and (c) of the Constitution of India, in the chapter on Directive Principles of State Policy, directs that the State shall ensure:-

(a) That the ownership and control of the material resources of the community are so distributed as best to sub serve the common good.

(b) That the operation of the economic system does not result in the concentration of wealth and means of production to the common detriment.[2]

The Central Government plays an advisory and coordinating role in the field of land reforms as the subject is under the exclusive legislative and administrative jurisdiction of the States as per the 7th Schedule of the Indian Constitution.[3]

The major objectives of land reforms consists of reordering agrarian relations to achieve an egalitarian social structure, to eliminate the exploitation in land relations and realising the age old goal of land to the actual tiller, thus enlarging the land base of the rural poor.

Meanwhile, right from the Colonial British period, the members of India's Communist Party of India (CPI) trained and organised by the Russian Communist party began working in the field in 1946. They started organising the lower caste agricultural workers and the Adivasis or forest tribes who were working as agricultural labour in the lands of the Upper castes in two areas of undivided India. The first was in North Bengal, in the districts of Rangpur, Dinajpur and later in 24 Parganas in undivided Bengal. Though the British Government had taken over the administration of the country in

---

[1] Naxalism, Causes and Cure Dr. P.K. Aggarwal, IAS, Manas Publications 2010.
[2] Ibid.
[3] Ibid.

1857, after they quelled the Sepoy mutiny, they did not materially interfere with the Revenue system of the country, except in some areas as mentioned above. It was the Communist party of India who studied the Revenue system in the country and took the first steps to rectify this. They probably tried to convince the Government to improve the land revenue system, but probably not finding any positive steps being taken decided to take the law into their own hands to correct the lop sided land ownership system.

The Tebagha Movementin North Bengal -1946

The system prevailing in Bengal at that time was for the land owners to make the lower caste agricultural labour cultivate their lands. The labour were allowed one fifth of the crop as their wages. The Communist Party of India (CPI) started the Tebagha Movement by organising agitations by the farm labour to increase their wages from one fifth of the crop to two third. They operated in three areas, of undivided Bengal-Rangpur, Dinajpur and 24 Parganas. They first formed *Kisan Sabhas* from among the labourers who were working in the farms of the rich upper classes. They then directed the cadres to forcibly take away two thirds of the paddy that had been stored by the landlords. Many landlords fled from their holdings. The CPI leaders had planned their operations carefully by withholding the information of the Kisan Sabhas operating against land lords whose holdings were in the interior. The landlords however soon regrouped and brought the Police to intervene. The police on getting information regrouped themselves and went into the interior villages and clashed with the labourers, organised to attack the landlords. The movement petered out as the Police reversed all the incidents of forcible occupation of good cultivable lands by the Kisan Sabha volunteers. In 1946, land ceiling laws had not yet been legislated. The action of the CPI in instigating and organising the farm labourers to act against the landlords was strictly illegal.

The Telengana Insurrection-1946-51

This movement was again organised by the CPI in the princely state of Hyderabad, then ruled by the Nizam. The British had never interfered with the Revenue system in the Princely states. In Hyderabad state, all the agricultural land was owned by landlords called *Doras and nawabs.* The Hindu *Doras* were all upper caste consisting of some Brahmins and two other dominant castes called *Reddy* and *Kamma*. Both were extremely arrogant and treated the lower caste and scheduled caste labourers like dirt. They owned vast tracts of cultivable land very often exceeding 1000 acres. The CPI cadres, incidentally all of upper castes began working in Telengana, with the lower caste labourers who worked on the lands of the *Doras*. In those days the districts were quite large and the police stations were few and far between. Working with the lower caste labourers the CPI workers instigated them to surround the houses of the *Doras*, armed with bows and arrows they forced them to part with portion of their land to be distributed among the labourers. In some places they looted the granaries of the landlords. The *Doras* reacted by getting the Police to visit the interiors and raid the villages of the lower caste workers, whenever clashes took place between the labourers and the Police, the Police won. At one time the CPI led lower caste labourers controlled more than 3000 villages. It was at about this time that the Nizam, the Muslim ruler of Hyderabad State refused to cede into India and the Indian Army was sent in to defeat the Nizam's forces. The Indian troops liberated Hyderabad after a struggle that lasted nearly seven months. The armed struggle of the CPI cadres against the upper caste landlords continued even after the Nizam's forces were defeated by the Indian Army. The Police gradually controlled the liberation struggle of the CPI cadres and finally the CPI called off the operation.

Naxalbari

Naxalbari in North Bengal's Darjeeling district is a small sleepy town nestling in the foothills of the Himalayas leading to Darjeeling. It was inhabited by Adivasi tribes- *Santhals, Oraons, Mundas, and Rajbongshis*. The tribals and scheduled castes were a majority of the population of Naxalbari, and two other villages Kharibari and Phansidewa also involved in the incidents that took place there. The tribals and scheduled castes were working as labourers in the farms, tea gardens and mines of the landlords. Among the farm labourers, all of them were *bagchashis* or tenant farmers. The *bagchashis* were exploited by the *jotedars* or landlords.

After the constitution was passed, the State Government passed the West Bengal Land Reforms Act in1955. When this was done the Jotedars started to make fake transfers to disguise their holdings above the notified ceiling. Seeing the malafide transfers being made by the Jotedars, to bypass the land reforms carried out by the Government, there was serious tension between the *Bagchashis (*tenant farmers*)* and the *Jotedars.* The Communist Party of India then intervened and organised Kisan Sabhas among the tenant farmers. It was at this time that a split occurred in the CPI and the Communist Party of India Marxist (CPM) was formed. The CPM captured most of the Kisan Sabhas. It was also at this stage that three leaders emerged in the movement around Naxalbari-Charu Majumdar, Kanu Sanyal and Jangal Santhal. The West Bengal *Kisan* conference was held in Burdwan in October 1966. This conference was to discuss what action was to be taken considering the way the Jotedars were trying to sideline the Land Ceiling legislation. Here, Charu Majumdar put forward a different line by talking of building liberated *Kisan* areas and organising partisan struggle. The Siliguri group on returning from Burdwan organised a separate Kisan Convention. They gave a call to:-

(a) Establish the authority of the peasant committee in all matters of the village.

(b) Get organised and be armed in order to crush the resistance of jotedars.

(c) Smash the jotedars monopoly of ownership of the land and redistribute the land through the peasant committees.[4]

This was like raising a battle cry. The pattern of events that followed was mostly shaped by Charu Majumdar, who was the brain, Kanu Sanyal, spread the organizational network and Jangal Santhal, mobilised the Santhals. They propagated that all the land of the landlords would be taken away and distributed among the kisans. The People's Daily of Communist China wrote on this- "Revolutionary peasents in the Darjeeling area have risen in rebellion. Under the leadership of a revolutionary group of the Indian Communist party a red area of rural revolutionary armed struggle has been established in India."[5]

Violent events followed this exhortation of Charu Majumdar. Santhals armed with bows and arrows occupied the lands of the kulaks and ploughed them to establish their ownership. Demonstrations were organised against

---

[4] Report on the peasant movement in the Terai Region. Kanu Sanyal. Liberation. November 1968.

[5] *Peoples Daily* Editorial. 5 July 1967.

hoarding of paddy by the kulaks. In some cases the entire stock was forcibly taken and distributed among the farmers or sold at cheaper rates. There were violent clashes. Between March and May 1967 nearly a hundred incidents were reported to the Police. The district authorities were initially hesitant to take action. Hare Krishna Konar, the Land Revenue Minister flew to Siliguri on 17 May and succeeded in bringing Kanu Sanyal to the conference table. In the meeting that followed it was agreed that lawless activities would be suspended, land distributed in consultation with the local agencies, stocks dehoarded on the basis of information supplied by the peoples committees and that all the wanted persons, including Jangal Santhal and Kanu Sanyal would surrender to the Police by a specified date. Kanu Sanyal however did not turn up as promised. The extremists decided to continue their movement. Meanwhile the Government decided to act firmly and directed the Police to arrest all the persons involved in violent activities. The Inspector who led the first Police party that went into the area was killed. Thereafter, the issue became violent. The Sub Divisional Officer who led the rescue party was encircled and he ordered his posse of policemen to fire on a riotous mob. Ten persons were killed, six of whom were women. This led to a massive deployment of Police forces. 1500 policemen were deployed and the movement was crushed.[6]

Regrettably, though the Constitution's Ninth Schedule had clearly laid out the path to be followed as regards agricultural land ownership, no attempt was made to effect land ceiling laws except for three States, Jammu and Kashmir, West Bengal and Kerala. In Jammu and Kashmir, Sheikh Abdullah who had taken over as the Chief Minister enforced land ceiling laws because he found that the majority of land lords were Hindus, while the farm labour were Muslims. The land ceiling laws enforced in Kashmir has held to the test of time. The only other states where legislated land ceiling laws were enforced on the ground were in West Bengal and Kerala, both held by Communist Ministries. In West Bengal, the Naxalbari outburst certainly played a part in the Land ceiling laws being enforced. The agitation did not go in vain!

---

[6] Prakash Singh, The Naxalite Movement in India, Rupa and Company, 1995.

There was a second fallout of the Naxalbari revolt by the exploited landless farmers. There was a split in the CPI M. There was a lot of rhetoric in the conclave of the CPI M at Madurai in August 1967. Instead of analysing the causes of the outburst by the farm labour in Naxalbari, and talking about the Indian Constitution's Ninth Schedule laying down the policy on Land Ceiling laws, the CPI M came out with a lot of rhetoric about a socialist state. Charu Majumdar retorted that Agrarian Revolution is the path forward. He wanted to set up revolutionary bases in rural areas, which would encircle the urban centres. This finally led to the formation of a new All India Coordination Committee at a meeting in Calcutta that was attended by extremists from several states. The Committee met again in May 1968 and changed its name to the All India Coordination Committee of Communist Revolutionaries (AICCR). The declaration underscored the semi-colonial and semi-feudal character of India and gave a call for Peoples Democratic Revolution. Finally on April 22, 1969 the AICCR declared its own liquidation and created the Communist Party of India Marxist-Leninist (CPI ML).

The political resolution of the CPI ML stated that India is a semi colonial and semi feudal country. The Indian State is a state of the big landlords and comprador bureaucrats....The principal contradiction in the country is between feudalism and the peasant masses....Guerilla warfare would be the basic tactic of struggle...The CPI ML would be a party of armed revolution. No other path exists before the Indian people but the path of armed revolution. Kanu Sanyal, announced the formation of the CPI ML at Calcutta on May first 1969. The Chinese Communist Party welcomed the formation of the CPI ML in India.

What was the reaction to the Government of India to this development? By this time West Bengal and Kerala had already legislated Land Ceiling legislations under the Ninth Schedule of the Constitution. Both these states had done this because the Communist Party of India Marxist was ruling in Kerala and was a coalition partner in West Bengal. In West Bengal the Naxalbari revolution took place because the Jotedars (land owners) tried to subvert the Land Ceiling act passed, by fake transfers of land to show that each land owner did not have land beyond the ceiling. It was the fault of the Revenue Administration of West Bengal that they did not see through the game of the Jotedars. In Kerala, when an attempt was made to start a

Naxal type insurgency, it did not take off because there was no cause for it, as by that time all tenant farmers had got ownership of their lands.

In this background it is inexplicable that the Government of India made no attempt to see that the states like Andhra Pradesh, Bihar were directed firmly to enforce the Land Ceiling laws that these States had also legislated by then.

Srikakulam

The insurgency in Srikakulam district of Andhra Pradesh began even before Naxalbari erupted. Srikakulam is in northeastern Andhra Pradesh, a hilly forested area, bordering Orissa and Madhya Pradesh, inhabited by mainly two tribes *Jatapu* and *Sayara*. These two tribes were commonly referred to as *Girijans*. They had been subjected to the most ruthless exploitation by traders and moneylenders, naturally belonging to the Vaisya community.

The *Girijans* were engaged in agriculture and in collecting forest produce, which they sold in the weekly *shandies* to the *bania* traders. The British had tried to protect the Girijans from being exploited by the caste Hindu *banias*. In 1917, they had directed that land could not be transferred from a Girijan to a non Girijan without the permission of the District Collector. This direction was unfortunately more in the breach than in favour of the *Girijans*. The *Bania* traders exploited the Girijans by fudging their account books and inflating the items given by them in exchange for the forest produce collected by the Girijans. When they could not repay them, *Banias* forcibly took away their lands. Gradually most of the fertile lands of the Girijans were taken away by the traders. The Girijans were thus reduced by the plainsmen to become labourers in their own country.

Andhra Pradesh passed its Land Ceiling legislation, under the Ninth Schedule of the Constitution in 1961-The Andhra Pradesh Ceiling on Agricultural Holding Act 1961. This was however never implemented on the ground unlike in West Bengal!

The landlords squeezed the farm labour to the utmost and paid subsistence wages to the farm labour and less than half a rupee to the daily wage earners. The tenant farmers had to give two thirds of the harvest to the landlords. It was at this stage that a savior came to the rescue of the Girijans. He was an upper caste Hindu, Vempatapu Satyanarayana. He came as a school teacher from the plains and settled in the Girijan area. Seeing the way the *Girijans* were being exploited, he began to organise them and forced the land owners and the contractors to pay fair wages to them. Coming up against the power of the upper classes, Vempatapu Satyanarayana had to give up his school teacher's job. Then he devoted his full time to working for the rights of the Girijans. He began to work for giving rights to the *Girijans* to cultivate wastelands, increasing the wages of farm labour, reduction in the landlord's share for crops cultivated, reduction of interest on loans given to Girijans, and ending of harassment by Forest and Police officials.

As a result of his work the wages of farm labour increased fivefold, 1600 to 2000 acres of land held in excess by landlords were forcibly wrested from them and given to landless farmers and 5000 odd acres of waste land were given to landless Girijans. The landlords' share of harvest of tenant farmers was reduced from two third to one third. Because of his good work the Girijans became politically conscious. Then on 31 October 1967, there was a clash between a large group of tribals and some landlords, who fired and killed two Girijans. The Girijan movement then became violent. Vempatapu Satyanarayana organised the Girijans into squads called *dalams*. The *dalams* armed with bows and arrows attacked the houses of landlords and money lenders. The Srikakulam group had joined the CPIM in 1964. In 1968, they broke away and joined the CPI ML. On 24 November, the Naxalites struck at Garudabhadra. A squad of women Girijans was obstructed by the landlord's men. That night, Vempatapu Satyanarayana organised an attack on the house of a landlord and looted property. Another group of about 250 Girijans forcibly harvested the standing crops of a landlord. A number of encounters with the Police ensued. In the period from December 1968 to 30 January 1969, 29 policemen were killed in action. Charu Majumdar visited Srikakulam in March 1969 which gave an instant fillip to the movement.

The Girijans claimed political power over 300 villages. Then on 11 October 1967, a procession of Girijans going for a meeting of the CPI ML was stopped by a group of landlords. In the ensuing clashes, the landlords used their guns, and killed two tribals. This resulted in the movement becoming violent. Vempatapu Satyanarayana immediately stepped in and organised dalams. The dalams conducted raids on *shandies*, attacked the houses of landlords, and money lenders and looted properties and food grains. The Police were reinforced and the Girijan dalams had their first encounter with the Police on 4 March 1968. Two Girijans were killed in the encounter.

This did not deter the Girijans. It was at this time that the Communist cadres in the dalams decided to leave the CPI M and join the All India Coordination Committee of Communist Revolutionaries (AICCCR). Soon thereafter, some members of the Srikakulam Committee went to Calcutta and met Charu Mazumdar. It was decided that an insurrection, as it happened in Srikakulam, should be organised in Andhra also. This was approved by the Srikakulam leaders-Vempatapu Satyanarayana, Panchai Krishnamurthy, Tahamada Ganapathi, M. Appalasuri and Tejeswara Rao at Bodapadu village in the plains area of Sompeta Taluk of Srikakulam. About a month later, the group struck at Garudabhadra. Here a group of women volunteers were preparing for a political demonstration, when they were obstructed and also manhandled by servants of the landlords. Reacting to this a group of Girijans of the Sompeta and Tekkali Taluks descended on the fields of a farmer and forcibly harvested the standing crop there. The same night, Vempatapu Satyanarayana led an attack on the house of a landlord. This was followed by a series of raids on the houses of landlords, money lenders and their agents in which they burnt down their houses and looted cash and other property. There were a number of encounters with the Police in which 29 policemen were killed. The area was in a sense liberated with the Girijans controlling at least 300 villages. About a hundred square miles of hilly terrain deep in the interior of Parvathipuram Agency was under the control of the Naxalites. It had become a Red area. In 1968, it was estimated that the Naxalites committed 23 murders and 40 dacoities in Srikakulam district. On 20 June 1969, about eighty armed Naxalites raided the house of a rich merchant Bhu Chandra Rao, and a woman Naxalite later identified as Panchadi Nirmala killed him.

A major Police operation was started in Srikakulam by end 1969. In an encounter in July 1969, in the Bori Hills of Parvathipuram, two top Naxalite leaders Vempatapu Satyanarayana and Adhibatla Kailasam were killed.

With their deaths, the tribal insurgency in Srikakulam petered out.

What is unfortunate about the insurgency in Srikakulam is that the State Government, had passed the Land Revenue Laws under the Ninth Schedule-The Andhra Pradesh ceiling on Agricultural Holding Act 1961 but did nothing to alleviate the genuine wants of its scheduled tribes. Instead the Revenue authorities were collaborating with the landlords or Doras against the scheduled tribes, not notifying land that was available to the Government in favour of the scheduled tribes of the district.

West Bengal-Midnapur and Birbhum

The Midnapur district of West Bengal borders Bihar and Orissa. The district has a sizeable population of tribals- Santhals Oraons and Lodhas. The majority of them were landless labourers, though a small proportion owned small plots of land or cultivated the *Jotedar's* land under the *Barga* system. Obviously as in Naxalbari, Kharibari and Phansideva the *Jotedars* had managed to circumvent the Land Ceiling legislation made by the State Government in 1955. After the Naxalbari uprising, a section of the CPI M workers began following the CPI ML line. They supported the *Bargadars* and *Kisans* during the harvest of 1967 and worked up a movement against the *Jotedars*. The remarkable part of this movement was the involvement of students from Calcutta University all from the well to do upper castes. Santosh Rana an MSc from Calcutta University took a job of a school teacher in Nayanbhasa Higher Secondary School under Gopibhallavpur Police Station. He organised the Santhals who were still landless despite the passing of the Land Ceiling Act in 1955 and incited them to seize the benami and vested lands of the jotedars and even loot paddy from their granaries.

The Midnapur district of West Bengal borders Bihar and Orissa. The district has a sizeable population of tribals, *Lodhas, Santhals and Oraons*. The majority of them were landless labourers, though a small proportion of them owned small plots of land or were *bargadars*. The operation of the West Bengal Land Revenue Act 1961 obviously had not yet been effected in these districts, giving the chance for the CPI ML to win over the tribals and make them take the law into their hands. After the Naxalbari uprising all the CPI M leaders of the area had come out and joined the CPI ML en bloc. The leading figures in the uprising in Debra were Bhabadeb Mondal an advocate and Gunadhar Murmu, a local tribal leader. It is interesting that in Gopibhallavpur, the leaders were Santosh Rana and Ashim Chatterjee, both products of Calcutta University, and both from upper castes, who were attracted by the way the lower castes were being exploited. Both these leaders organised the Bargadars against the Jotedars, to seize their *benami* lands and even loot paddy from their granaries, paddy that had been harvested by the *bargadars* and taken in disproportionate quantity by the *jotedars*. What was remarkable was the way the city bred young students completely identified themselves with the tribals.

In Debra, the movement started with demands to raise wages of agricultural labourers. Santosh Rana took up a job of a school teacher in Nayanbasan Higher Secondary school and started meetings of landless Santhals and incited them to rise in revolt against the capitalist *jotedars,* seize their benami vested lands and even loot paddy from their granaries. Ashim Chatterjee also followed, working among landless labour. The upper castes students from Calcutta University completely identified with the landless tribals. The CPI ML then organised a series of raids on the houses of money lenders and jotedars. Class enemies were killed, their property and arms were looted, and stocks of food grains lifted and distributed among the poor and landless peasents. Twelve big landlords were killed during October, November 1967 in the Gopiballavpur area. On 1 October 1969, a mob of a thousand Adivasis led by Gunadhar Murmu surrounded the house of Kanai Kuity, a *Jotedar.* He escaped, but the mob ransacked his house after recovering all the land documents and burnt them. In subsequent raids, three other jotedars were killed. All this could only mean one thing. ACPIM government had been elected and was in power. They had taken action to see that the provisions of the West Bengal Land Reforms Act under the Ninth Schedule of the Constitution had been effected on the ground in Naxalbari area. There the jotedars had tried to bypass the act by illegally transferring there excessive holdings. In the case of the jotedars of Midnapur, they must have done the same thing. It was thus a clear failure of the Revenue administration of the district. What is not explicable is the reaction of the Central Government. It is right that they took action to quell a leftist rebellion, but why did they not apply their mind as to where the failure was. After all it is the Centre which framed the Ninth amendment to the

Constitution, which led to the passing of the Land Reforms Acts in different States. The whole CPI ML revolution in different states could have been averted if the Government at the Centre and the States took action to see that the land reforms were effected on a war footing.

Despite the fact that a CPI M Government was ruling in West Bengal, and that they had already issued orders for implementing the provisions of the Land Reforms Act passed in the State, the Jotedars either did not comply or tried to do malafide transfers as in the case of Naxalbari. That is why the Santhal CPI ML leader Gunadhar Murmu issued a *gera* after the traditional tribal custom of tying a knot on the bark of the Sal tree, symbolizing revenge and called upon his followers to take severe action against the jotedars and district officials. The campaign of the CPI ML groups continued till 1970. At least four more jotedars who had apportioned large tracts of land were killed by the CPI ML organised gangs. The Centre then dismissed the CPI M government and enforced Presidents rule. When President's rule was enforced, the Police got a free hand and operated vigorously against the CPI ML sponsored groups and controlled the situation.

The reaction of the State was to send in three more companies of Armed Force and in the operations about 300 extremists were arrested. The top leadership however eluded the forces and escaped. The movement in Birbhum virtually collapsed under the onslaught of the different forces sent to the area.

Bihar and Uttar Pradesh

The action of the peasants in Naxalbari had enthused the landless and tenant farmers of Bihar and Uttar Pradesh. In the Mushahari block of Muzzafarpur district in Bihar, there were 12 villages with a population of 10,000 people. There were disputes between the landlords and the tenant farmers over occupancy rights. Above everything else, the peasantry nursed a grievance against the landlords of being subjected to several kinds of social oppression. In April 1968, the peasants of Gangapur harvested the *arahar* crop of the landlord in broad daylight. Bijli Singh the *zamindar* of Narsinghpur organised an attack on the peasents with 300 men armed with lathis, swords and guns. Bijli Singh on an elephant led the attack. In a fight that lasted four hours, Bijli Singh and his gang of thugs were defeated and they fled in disarray.

The humbling of this powerful landlord by poor farmers mostly scheduled castes had a great impact on the surrounding villages. *Kisan Sangram Samitis* (Peasents Action Committees) were quickly organised in most of the villages as also *Gram Rakshak Dals* (Village Defence Squads). This movement was however quickly crushed by firm Police action. Regrettably, there was also considerable repression in the Police action, with farmers being arrested, their huts burned and properties destroyed. This not only drove the Naxal leaders underground, but also resulted in a backlash by the Naxal groups.

In April 1969, there was a clash in a village Lakhanuari of Paru Police Station. Landless peasents forcibly harvested the crop on 14 acres of land of a landlord. The landlord's retainers retaliated with guns and *lathis* but were beaten back. The peasants also killed one of the landlord's retainers. In June 1969, an organised group of peasents attacked a landlord who had land far in excess of the ceiling and was also a moneylender, taking the ornaments of the peasants as security. The mob led by the Naxal workers killed the landlord and two of his lieutenants seized all deeds and documents of lands of poor farmers that he had seized in lieu of non repayment of loans and also recovered dozens of ornaments that had been pledged to the landlord by poor peasants. Hundreds of peasants gathered after the raid and in their presence the Naxal leaders burnt all the land deeds and returned all the pawned ornaments to their owners. After this the Naxal leaders raided the house of Bijli Singh and killed him.

In August 1968, the farmers of Harikesh village seized some land from a landlord. He sought police help and a villager was arrested. The farmers reacted, collected in a group and assaulted the landlord and got the arrested peasant released. This was followed by massive repression as the police set up a camp in the area. The villagers were assaulted, and their houses burnt. All the villagers at the receiving end became destitute. The Naxalite leaders went underground.

The states reaction was that the Police was activated and reinforcements obtained and extensive combing operations carried out. The movement gradually faded out. During investigations, interrogation was done and suspects were arrested, it emerged that Naxal leaders from West Bengal had infiltrated in the area and organised the movement and trained the selected cadres.

The movement also spread to Dharbanga, Champaran districts and to the Chota Nagpur area. In operations conducted in these areas 54 Naxal cadres all Adivasis of the area were arrested. The trouble then spread to Singhbum and Ranchi districts, and Jamshedpur city was seriously affected. Ranchi town was also badly affected.

The Palia area of Uttar Pradesh borders the Terai area of Nepal. It is densely forested and inhabited by Tharu tribals. The State Government had undertaken a project for clearing the forests and encouraged poor peasents from eastern Uttar Pradesh to come to the area, clear the forests and set up farmland. As these poor peasents cleared the land, rich farmers descended on the area, pushed out the peasents and occupied big tracts of cleared land. The hard labour of the poor peasents went in vain. Attracted by their plight, the Naxals descended on the area and began to organise the poor peasents who had been cheated of their hard labour. The Naxal movement however did not develop as strongly as it did in Bihar or West Bengal.

Operation Steeple Chase

With Naxalite trouble spreading to Bihar and Orissa, the Central Government decided to take strong action to crush this leftist movement. The Bureaucracy does not seem to have advised the Central Government of the causes of agrarian unrest, of the non implementation of the enactments of the Ninth Schedule and the exploitation by the landlord upper classes of the scheduled castes and tribal farmers, who were being forced to work for subsistence wages in the lands of the upper classes whose holdings were well above the land ceiling prescribed in the Land Reforms Acts legislated on the basis of the Ninth Schedule of the Constitution. All these Land Reform Acts were passed in the early 1950s.

Induction of Army

The Central Government was only focusing on the growth of the CPI ML, not emphasizing the fact that it was the exploitation by the upper class landlords of the poor landless farmers, denying land to them that was feeding the CPI ML. After spread of Naxal activity from West Bengal to Bihar and Uttar Pradesh, the Central Government planned an interstate operation, in which for the first time the Army was called in, though only to establish an outer cordon in a joint operation covering the border areas of West Bengal, Bihar and Orissa. The CRPF formed the inner cordon and the Police forces of the three states operated inside the villages and towns. The operation was conducted from 1 July to 15 August 1971. It covered Midnapur, Purulia, Birbhum and Burdwan districts of West Bengal, Singhbum, Santhal Parghanas and Dhanbad districts of Bihar and Mayurbhanj of Orissa. Besides, a Congress Government had been elected in West Bengal and under a rightist Chief Minister, extra judicial methods were freely adopted to crush the Leftist movement. In West Bengal, the CPI M ministry had effected the Land Reforms Act passed in 1955, but as in the case of Naxalbari, the Jotedars in Midnapur and other southern districts also tried to bypass the directions of the Land Reforms Act. The tenant farmers and landless people, organised by the CPI ML cadres therefore took the law into their own hands and attacked the landlords and their hired thugs. While taking action against the unlawful acts of the landless peasants and the tenants cheated of their rights by the Jotedars, the Government did not care to see that the laws of the land were being enforced, but gave in to the landlord lobby.

The Prime Minister, Mrs. Indira Gandhi stated in the Rajya Sabha on 11 August 1970 that the Government was committed to putting down the activities of the Naxalites, with all the strength at its command. These elements would be fought to the finish, she said. Operation Steeple Chase in July August 1971 had already broken the backbone of the Naxalites in the worst affected bordering areas of Bihar and West Bengal. In the first quarter of 1972, almost all the top Naxalite leaders had been apprehended by the Police, Kanu Sanyal, Jangal Santhal, Nagabushanam Patnaik, Kunnikal Narayanan and Ashim Chatterjee. Charu Majumdar was also arrested and died in prison. About 1400 Naxalites were in jail in Andhra Pradesh, 2000 in Bihar and about 4000 in West Bengal. These were not educated motivated Communist cadres, but landless peasents and tenant farmers who were denied their constitutional rights as per the Land Reforms Acts legislatedas per the Ninth Schedule of the Constitution and roused by the Naxalite leaders to fight for their rights. They had of course committed unlawful acts, but no one in Government ever asked why they had taken to violence against their oppressive landlords. The answers were clear, as if written on a wall in bold letters, but the Government did not want to do anything to set right age old wrongs against its poor scheduled castes and tribes. The bogey was the CPI ML leading the movement and the fear that if they came to power, that would be the end of the rule of the upper castes, with their unlimited ownership of land and continued exploitation of the scheduled castes and tribes.

Consider the oppression of the lower castes in Bihar. In Bhojpur district of Bihar, the lower castes lived in utter poverty and were also subjected to social exploitation. Kalyan Mukherjee and Rajender Singh Yadav described that the oppression of the lower castes at the hands of the upper castes did not flow from numerical superiority, but rather from niches in the economic hierarchy apropos land ownership and the monopoly over labour. Further the culture of violence ensured that the *Chamar* or the *Musahar* never raise their heads in protest. Though *begar* was a thing of the past, the *banihar* worked often for nothing. Wearing a clean dhoti, remaining seated in the presence of the master, even on a cot outside his own hut, walking erect were taboo. When the evenings fell or in lonely stretches of field, the rape of his womenfolk by the landlord's *lathieths* and scions complete a picture of unbridled *Bumihar, Rajput* over lordship.

It is therefore clear that though the Central Government had to some extent crushed the CPI ML leftist movement, the root causes were not looked into by the Government and the oppressed classes continued to sullenly suffer the oppression of the upper classes.

Peoples War Group (PWG) in Andhra Pradesh, Madhya Pradesh and Maharashtra

It must be remembered that it was in North Bengal and the Telengana region of present Andhra Pradesh that the Communist Party of India first worked among the oppressed lower castes and Scheduled Tribes. It was in Andhra Pradesh that the leftist movement surfaced in the nineteen eighties. After Charu Mazumdar died, his colleagues Kondapalli Seetharamiah, K.G.Satyamurthy and Suniti Kumar Ghosh formed a Central Organising Committee in 1972. Of these three leaders, Kondapalli Seetharamiah, after release from jail, began to organise the workers. A series of robberies ensued, money that was used for keeping the cadres alive. On 20 April 1980, Kondapalli Seetharamiah, broke away from the Central Organising Committee of the CPI ML and formed the CPI ML Peoples War Group. In the next ten years, the Peoples War Group dominated the fight of the scheduled castes and tribes for justice, on land and forests emerging as the strongest leftist group in the country.

The Telengana region had already seen Naxalite activity, but its resurgence is due to the continued exploitation of the tribals by the landlords, traders and Government officials, especially those of the Forest Department. As P.S.Sundaram said, the tribals owning small plots of land are expropriated and sharecroppers impoverished. They are all kept under perpetual bondage, towards repayment of a small debt, supposedly taken generations ago. Forest wealth is freely smuggled out by contractors with the connivance of the forest staff. The tribals get neither a remunerative price for their forest produce nor a fair wage for their labour.[7]

The social dimensions of exploitation were far more revolting. The landlords of the region belonging to the Reddy and Velama community were addressed as *Dora*. The tyranny of *Doras* in Telengana was unmatched. *Dasi*, a film by Narsing Rao, depicts the life of a woman slave who enters the household of a *Dora* as part of the dowry of his bride. She is at the disposal of the master and his guests and she is forced to have abortions. She has to subsist on what is left over that the cook pleases to pass on.

On 20 May 1981, the Naxal leaders had called for a meeting at Indraveli and more than 30,000 Gond tribals turned up. Apprehending a clash between tribals and upper classes, the district administration refused permission. The Gond tribals decided that they would have the meeting. The Police took action to disperse the crowd. There was a lathi charge and then firing and thirteen Gond tribals were killed. Kondapalli Seetharamiah, th CPI ML leader was arrested on 2 January 1982, but managed to escape from the hospital ward of the Osmania hospital in Hyderabad. He then concentrated on organising the cadres and set up Forest Committees for the forest areas and Regional Committees for the plains areas. He formed armed squads or dalams of ten members each. Soon there were nearly fifty such dalams operating in Telengana area.

---

[7] Extent of Naxalite Revolt in Andhra Pradesh. V.M.Nair *Statesman,* 9 December 1969.

Kondapalli Seetharamiah, then set up several front organisations of the Peoples War Group. These were the Radical Students Union, Radical Youth League, Rythu Coolie Sangham, Mazdoor Kisan Sanghatan and Mahila Sravanthi. Besides these he set up the Singareni Karmika Samiti as the Trade Union Front and the Jana Natya Mandali as the cultural Front of the Peoples War Group. After organising these front organisations, Seetharamiah embarked on a clear course of action. These were redistribution of land, enforcing payment of minimum wages to farm labour, imposing taxes and penalties, holding Peoples Courts, destroying Government property, kidnapping Government functionaries, attacking Policemen and enforcing a social code.

The PWG is reported to have distributed nearly half a million acres of land across Andhra Pradesh, by forcibly occupying the excessive land of land owners and redistributing the land held in excess of the land authourised under the Andhra Pradesh Land Reforms Act-The Andhra Pradesh ceiling on Agricultural Holding Act 1961 to landless labour. When the Government deployed Police Forces to quell the excesses committed by the PWG *dalams*, the State Government filed an affidavit in the court listing out the cases of illegal distribution of land taken forcibly from the landlords by the PWG dalams. This was the affidavit No.68 of 1982. This stated that the Naxalite cadres had forcibly taken away land from different landlords totaling 80,000 acres of agricultural land, and 1,20,000 acres of forest land. It is strange that when filing this affidavit, the State Government forgot to mention that the land owners were holding excess land and the provisions of the Andhra Pradesh Land Reforms Act 1961 had not been enforced, and this was what the PWG had organised, due to the failure of the Government to enforce the laws that they had passed in their Assembly! The PWG cadres meanwhile had also forced the landlords to increase the daily wages from Rs. 15 to Rs. 25 and the annual wages for yearlong labour (*jeetagadu*) from Rs.2000 to Rs. 4000.

This forced agrarian justice brought about a sea change in the feudal system prevailing in the Telengana region. The poorer sections were very happy at these measures. They found that what the politicians had been talking about and the government promising year after year could be translated into a reality only after the intervention of the Naxalites-*Gorakala*

*Doras (*Lord of the Bushes*),* as the Naxalites were known in the interior forest areas.

The judgement in this case was extraordinary. The Government had not submitted that they had failed to enforce the Andhra Pradesh Land Reforms Act 1961, but only stated that the Naxalites had forcibly taken away land of the landlords. The court when deciding the case directed that the land taken away from the land lords be forcibly taken from the Naxalites and returned to the landlords. The honourable court forgot that in the first instance it was the State that had failed the people of the country in not enforcing the Land Ceiling as per the Andhra Pradesh Land Reforms Act legislated in pursuance of the Ninth Schedule of the Constitution. It was this lacuna that led to the creation of the Naxalites and the solution to this was the enforcement of the Land Reform Laws legislated. The sad conclusion is that there was no justice for the downtrodden in this land and even the Judiciary had joined the executive in oppressing the downtrodden. If this is the case then to whom will the downtrodden and oppressed classes turn to for justice? The only conclusion that one can come to is that it is the State, by its illegal actions that has led to the creation of the Peoples War Group!

It was during this period that the PWG managed to get fifty AK-47 rifles from the LTTE. During the N.T.Rama Rao Telugu Desam government, the PWG fought a running battle with them. They also spread its network to the coastal areas and Rayalseema districts of Andhra Pradesh. It then spread to the adjoining areas of Madhya Pradesh, Maharashtra and Orissa. In 1992, the State reorganised the anti Naxal operations and during sustained operations killed 248 Naxal cadres and arrested Kondapalli Seetharamiah. More than 8000 cadres surrendered before the Police.

It was in the early years of the 1990s that the Andhra Police raised the Greyhounds; a force specialized in Counter guerilla operations. The new force was raised by a former Chief Instructer of a specialised agency of the Government of India. The emphasis of the force was in developing expertise in Field craft and Tactics. As the Armed Police cadres inducted the Greyhounds and the Police officers and men were trained, the improvement in counter guerilla operations were immediately seen. The Greyhounds and the Andhra Police officers and men trained in Guerilla warfare courses made an immediate impact in anti Naxal operations. The Naxal groups were gradually pushed into Chhattisgarh Madhya Pradesh and Orissa and the situation normalised in the Telengana region.

Madhya Pradesh

The tribal district of Bastar was a sleepy forest outpost when the Naxals of Andhra Pradesh spilled over into their area after being hard pressed by the newly trained Greyhounds. The Adivasis of this area were subdued into a state of supine submission through years of subjugation. The Peoples Union for Civil Liberties a front organisation of the Naxalites found that through years of degradation, the Adivasis had become meek and submissive and had accepted that they were to be at the mercy of the upper castes forever. Organising the beaten down Adivasis, the Naxalites made them conscious of their rights and soon the meek and submissive Adivasis of Madhya Pradesh were standing up for their rights. The Peoples Union for Civil Liberties punished the corrupt officials, made the tendu leaf contractors to increase the wage rates. Unfortunately, the administration like in all the other states began to harden their stand and increasingly resorted to police action to restrain the Naxal cadres, ignoring the basic issues of rights to the forest of lakhs of Adivasis who were living in the forests for thousands of years. The leftist leadership had by now found a very good sanctuary in the Abujmad forests of south Chhattisgarh's Bijapur district.

Maharashtra

Gadchiroli in Maharashtra has a tribal population of 38 per cent. Two thirds of the state is thickly forested and the entire life and culture of the tribals revolves around the forests, but tragically, the tribals were denied access to the forests by a myopic interpretation of the Forest laws. The forest areas of the state should have been administered by the Governor by establishing a Tribal Advisory Council as per the Fifth Schedule of the Constitution. No Governor made any attempt to appoint a Tribal Advisory Council. The State had no power to administer the forests. It was then that the Naxal cadres from Andhra Pradesh took over matters and managed to get forests cleared for the tribals to live and earn their livelihood from the forests.

There were 113 incidents of Naxal violence in 1990 with 15 deaths. There were several incidents of landmines blasting Police vehicles and resultant casualties. This was basically because of lack of expertise in Counterinsurgency operations. With the deployment of the Indo Tibetan Border Police and the Border Security Force such incidents came down. The State and the Centre, however, have not touched the real issue. This is that the fifth Schedule of the Constitution has not been implemented in Maharashtra. No Governor has set up a Tribal Advisory Council and administered the Forest areas. The State Government has been illegally operating all these years and continues to do so. Why does the Government not implement the laws of the land? Further the State is violating another law passed- the Panchayat Extension to Scheduled Areas Act, by which the Tribals living in the forest should elect a Panchayat and this Panchayat, should decide how their forest is to be administered. How long does the Government want to use the Police and Para Military forces to crush the Naxalites and the Tribals by continuing their illegal and unlawful administration of the Forests?

Bihar

Bihar was a state where there was complete suppression of the Scheduled castes and tribes by the upper castes comprising the *Bumihars* and *Rajputs*. These two castes were landlords and extremely arrogant in their attitude to the scheduled castes and tribes. They considered that it was their birthright to own land and the Scheduled castes and tribes were born to live as serfs. With this arrogant attitude it was not a surprise to see the Communist party working among the landless Scheduled castes and tribes. This manifested in the form of three Naxalite groups in Bihar in the beginning of 1980-the Maoist Communist Centre, the CPI ML anti Lin Piao group and the CPI ML Party Unity. The movement grew rapidly in the face of the corrupt, casteist and incompetent administration.When the CPI ML was formed after the dissolution of the All India Coordination Committee of Communist Revolutionaries and the merger of several Maoist groups, one Naxalite group *Dakshin Desh* retained its distinct entity. The group chose Jangal Mahal of Burdwan district of West Bengal as its area of operation. This district had a sizeable tribal population. The terrain was full of forests, agricultural land was inadequate and the wage rates abysmally low. The landlords were all from the upper castes, while the scheduled castes and tribe were share croppers. These factors were ideal for launching a Maoist struggle. The

CPI ML had 37 militia and propaganda squads operating in this area by 1973. The squads killed several oppressive land owners, snatched weapons and were very active initially in Jangal Mahal area but soon spilled over into Bihar in Aurangabad and Gaya districts. In 1975, the group renamed itself as the Maoist Communist Centre (MCC). They soon spread over to the Central Bihar districts and reached strength of 10,000 members, with an armed wing the *Lal Raksha Dal* and managed to stockpile about 900 weapons including a few AK 47 Rifles. The MCC then embarked on an orgy of violence against the Rajputs and related upper castes. There were massacres of the upper castes in Baghaura and Dalelchak villages. Here, on 29 May 1987, 42 Rajputs both men and women were slaughtered with a venom resulting from years of oppression. A similar brutal massacre took place on 12 February 1992 in Bara village of Gaya district, where 37 members of the Bumihar landowning caste were hacked to death in an orgy of violence lasting four hours. Hundreds of years of caste oppression led to this orgy of violence. It was more a case of caste oppression rather than denial of land rights. This led to the creation of a number of private armies, each one dedicated to defending, their caste bastions. These were the *Bhumi Sena* of the *Kurmis* a land owning class, the *Lorik Sena* of the *Yadavs*, a supressed caste group, the *Brahmarishi sena* of the *Bumihars*, the *Lal Raksha Dal* of the MCC, and the *Lal Sena* of the anti Lin Piao faction, and the *Mazdoor KisanSangram Samiti* of the CPI ML. The MCC also held several *Jan Adalat* or Peoples Courts in which oppressive land lords were given the death penalty which was immediately carried out by chopping off the head of the landlord.

There were internecine conflicts between the different Naxal groups in Bihar over spheres of influence. The CPI ML Anti Lin Piao Liberation Group headed by Vinod Misra operated in Central Bihar and had about fifty underground armed squads armed with an assortment of weapons including some AK 47s'. In 1990 they were responsible for killing some 40 persons of the upper castes in 106 incidents.

The Naxal Fire Spreads

The first phase of Naxal violence was in the Srikakulam uprising in 1967 and the Naxalbari incidents in 1968. This phase ended with the death of

Charu Majumdar in 1972. The second phase of Naxal violence started with the formation of the Peoples War Group in Andhra Pradesh in 1980 and ended in the mid nineties with the expulsion of Kondapalli Seetharamiah and also the success of the new counterinsurgency force raised by the state of Andhra Pradesh. The third phase started with the holding of the Ninth Congress of the Peoples War Group in 2001.

The period from mid 1970 to the middle of 1971 saw maximum Naxalite violence, with some 4000 odd incidents taking place with killings of 565 people. After the death of Charu Majumdar, the quantum of violence came down and in 1981 there were only 325 incidents with 92 deaths. Then the Peoples War Group was formed in Andhra Pradesh under Kondapalli Seetharamiah and the movement spread in Andhra Pradesh and other states and in 1991 there were 1876 incidents with 474 killings. In 2001 there were 1208 incidents and 564 killings. During 2004, the worst affected states were Bihar, Chhattisgarh and Jharkhand. The Peoples War Group and the Maoist Communist Centre accounted for 90 Percent of the violence in the country. During 2005 till end October, as stated by the Union Home Minister in Parliament there were 1353 incidents of Naxalite violence with 570 deaths of civilians and Police personnel. The number of incidents was 448 in Andhra Pradesh, 317 in Chhattisgarh, 271 in Jharkhand, 161 in Bihar and 76 in Maharashtra.

Andhra Pradesh

By 2006, this state had the largest presence of Naxal insurgents and though the PWG was banned by the State and the PWG and the MCC were declared terrorist organisations by the centre under the Prevention of Terrorism Act 2002, it hardly affected the strike capability of the PWG or the MCC. The PWG was estimated to have 54 *dalams* with nearly 1100 fulltime cadres.

On 2 December 1999, three top leaders of the PWG, Nalla Adi Reddy, E.Santosh Reddy and Seelam Naresh were killed in the Koyyuru forest of Andhra Pradesh. Human Rights Group alleged that they were actually arrested by the Andhra Police in Bangalore on 1 December, flown in a helicopter to Hyderabad, interrogated there, and then taken to Koyyuru Reserve Forest and shot in a false encounter. The PWG retaliated with vengeance. On 15 December, Lakhiram Kavre, a minister in Madhya Pradesh was killed in Balaghat. Then on 18 February, the PWG attacked a police station in Vishakapatnam and killed 10 policemen. Then, on 20 February, the Naxalites struck in Bastar district of Madhya Pradesh, blowing up a police truck killing 23 policemen. Then, on 4 June, they attacked the State Bank of Hyderabad branch in Dhandapadu village of Nalgonda district and looted nine kilograms of gold worth Rs. 5 million. The most audacious attack of the PWG was the attempt to kill the Andhra Pradesh Chief Minister, Chandra Babu Naidu by detonating a Claymore mine that they had fixed at shoulder height on a hill road between Tirupati and Tirumala in Chitoor district. Earlier in March, the State Minister Madhava Reddy was killed in a similar blast at Ghatkesar near Hyderabad.

By now the PWG had spread to several States. In Bihar it had its presence in Patna, Aurangabad, Jehanabad, Gaya, Rohtas, Saharsha, Buxar, Khagaria, Banka and Jamui. In Jharkahand, it had units in Palamau, Garhwa, Lateha, Gumlam, Hazaribagh and Koderma. It had also spread to Orissa in Malakngiri, Koraput, Gajapati, Rayagarh, Nowrangpur and Mayurbhanj. It had spread in the districts of Jagdalpur, Bastar, Kanker, and Dantewada in Chhattisgarh. In West Bengal it became a challenge to the CPM in Midnapur, Purulia and Bankura districts.

The Congress Government elected in May 2004 lifted the ban on the Peoples War Group and its frontal organisations, the Radical Students Union, Radical Youth League, Singareni Karmikhya Samakhya, All India Revolutionary Students Federation, Dandakarnya Adivasi Kisan Mazdoor Sanghatan and Andhra Pradesh Ryuthu Coolie Sangam on 22 July 2004. Peace talks were held from 15 to 18 October. The Naxals presented a 11 point charter of demands, the most important related to land reforms. The Naxals called for an independent Commission to be headed by a democrat acceptable to all to identify land for distribution among the landless people. This was the crucial point and the Congress party in power could not agree on this, as their vote bank was among the landed class. Since, there were differences the talks were adjourned. It was at this stage that the PWG and the Maoist Communist Centre (MCC) merged on 21 September 2004 to form the Communist Party of India Maoist. This was however announced to the public on 14 October 2004. The peace talks held between 15 to 18 October 2004 was between the new CPI Maoist and the Congress

Government of Andhra Pradesh.

Shortly after, the Maoists attacked the Chilkaluripeta Police Station and killed four Policemen on 11 March 2005, to avenge the killing of ten Maoists in Nizamabad district on 7 March. On 17 August 2005, the State Government reinforced the ban on the Communist Party of India Maoist and its seven front organisations.

Bihar and Jharkand

Bihar was the worst administered state in India, riven by castes and where the upper castes treated the lower castes worse than dirt. It was the Maoist Communist Centre (MCC) that operated in this state. It is a known fact that Lalloo Prasad Yadav, a former Chief Minister of Bihar openly sided with the MCC during the elections of 1995 and was seen on the dais with several Yadav MCC leaders during the election campaign. It was at this time that a violent group was organised by the land owning upper caste of Bihar, the *Bumihars*. This armed group came to be known as the *Ranbhir Sena*. It was this group that carried out the worst massacre of the lower castes in Bathe Lakshmanpur village on 1 December 1997, butchering 67 people including 33 women and 13 children all reported to be supporters of the CPI ML in Bihar. I was Director General of the Border Security Force and after a meeting with the Home Secretary had sent a wireless detachment with the Inspector General of Communications to help the Bihar Police improve their wireless Communications. He came back and reported that the Central forces sent to Bihar Police instead of chasing the Ranbir Sena, who had killed innocent landless villagers, who had given food to a big party of CPI ML cadres, who had come to their village at night, began to hunt the CPI ML group! Several more killings and counter killings took place in Bihar. On 18 March 1999 thirty five upper caste persons were butchered by cadres of the Maoist Communist Centre (MCC) in Senari village of Jehanabad district. Then on 16 June 2000 the Ranvir Sena gunned down 35 persons including 14 women and 6 children of the Yadav community at Mianpur village of Aurangabad district. On 14 April 2001, the MCC cadres butchered 14 villagers of Belpu village of Hazaribagh district. The Naxal movement in Bihar turned into a violent caste war.

The MCC then shifted its focus to the Jharkand area, which by the way had been separated from Bihar as Jharkand State on 15 November 2000. Tribals of Jharkand are 27 percent of the population of the State. Jharkand is a heavily forested State. Out of 22 districts of Jharkand the Naxalites are reported to be active in 15. These are Palamau, Giridh, Garwa, Chatra, Latehar, Ranchi, Gumla, Hazaribagh, Lohardanga and Bokaro. Since the district is heavily forested, and the forest roads are mostly rough roads without surface tar, it is heavily mined and Para military forces moving on these country roads in forested areas have suffered heavy casualties while their buses and trucks were blown off. The MCC even blew off several mine proof vehicles, by cleverly burying the mine under the road and activating the mine as this heavy vehicle drove over the buried mine. On each occassion, the MCC cadres buried more than 50 kilograms of the explosive under the road.

On 7 May 2002, 15 Police personnel were killed in a landmine blast during an economic blockade. On 20 November 2002, eight security force personnel were killed. On 20 December 2002, 14 Jharkand Policemen were killed in an ambush by the MCC in Saramda forest in West Singhbum district. On 18 March 2003, the MCC attacked the Police post in Lodipur village of Gaya district and looted 15 rifles and 1000 rounds of ammunition. On 14 April 2003, about 150 cadres of the MCC attacked a Police post in Chanerapura railway station in Bokaro district and looted 23 rifles and several hundred rounds of ammunition. There were a number of women cadres in this attack. On 15 April 2003, MCC cadres activated a land mine in the Cherki Valley forest of Nawada District. Eight Police personnel were killed and the MCC looted 2 rifles, 6 SLR's and several rounds of ammunition.

Mining activity in the Jharkand forests was badly affected by the activities of the MCC cadres, who extorted money from the officials of the mines by kidnapping them and releasing them for ransom. They also taxed the trucks transporting coal. On 11 December 2003, the MCC cadres committed a dacoity in the office of the Indian Aluminium Company and looted Rs. 1,04,000. On 7 April, 2004, the MCC killed 27 Policemen in a land mine blast in Baliwa village under Gua Police station in West Singhbum district.

Madhya Pradesh and Chhattisgarh

Madhya Pradesh was bifurcated in November 2000. Except for a few districts in Madhya Pradesh, it is Chhattisgarh that had become a centre of Naxal operations. In Bastar district, an Additional SP and twenty two Policemen were killed in a land mine explosion on 20 February 2000. The People's War Group came into Chhattisgarh area when they were hard pressed by the new Armed Police group raised by the Andhra Pradesh Police, the Greyhounds. Trained by a former Chief Instructer of Guerilla warfare, it is the best force among all Central and State forces to operate against the Naxal groups. When the PWG group retreated into Chhattisgarh, they found the local Adivasis quite passive and did not succeed too well in arousing them to be trained and fight the oppressive Government. Many refused to go for training to fight the Government and when the PWG began to force them, they fled to the urban areas to avoid training. An enterprising *Adivasi* who had joined the Congress party then succeeded in organising them as a counter Guerilla force. This was the origin of the *Salwa Judum* which has since been found to be betraying the tribal cause for equality.

The PWG spread its area of operations to the Bastar region, which includes four districts, Bijapur, Bastar, Dantewada and Kanker. During the year 2003, there were 103 encounters in which 31 police personnel were killed. The Peoples War Group and the Maoist Communist Centre were active in 96 Police stations in 7 districts of the State. On 7 May 2005, the Naxals attacked the offices of the Hindalco Industries in Saridih in Surguja district. On 3 September, 2005, the CRPF hit a landmine at Kupjernala in Bijapur district and lost 22 personnel. In this area, the PWG cadres were found discouraging the Adivasis from worshipping Hindu and Christian Gods. Today after the disastrous ambush of five platoons of the CRPF, in Dantewada in 2010, in which 86 personnel were killed, it is the district that has had the maximum casualties of Security personnel.

Odisha

Odisha has some of the poorest districts of the country, where the Tribal belt is marked by exploitation of the have-nots. To add to the misery, the governance is poor and the Police ill trained to handle this problem. The

PWG was active in Malkangiri, Rayagada, Gajapati, Ganjam, Koraput and Nabrangpur districts bordering Andhra Pradesh. The MCC operated in Mayurbhanj, Keonjhar and Sundergarh, bordering Jharkhand. On 9 August 2001, 230 cadres of the PWG carried out daring coordinated raids on the Kalimela and Motu Police Stations of Malkangiri districts killing 6 Policemen and succeeded in taking away a substantial number of weapons and hundreds of rounds of ammunition. On 5 December 2002, the PWG triggered a landmine and blew up a vehicle of the Orissa Special Armed Police, injuring 18 of their personnel. In the same month, the PWG carried out a series of attacks on houses of rich farmers, private granaries, and some government godowns, looted some 1000 quintals of rice, which they later distributed among poor tribals. In April 2003, the PWG cadres looted some 550 kilograms of explosives from the Sundergarh district of Odisha and moved across into the Saranda forests of West Singhbum district of Jharkand. On 30 July 2003, the PWG triggered a landmine in the Vejingiwada forest in Malakngiri district when a CRPF truck was passing through a forest road killing 5 CRPF and 5 State Police personnel. The PWG conducted a major attack on 7 February 2004, overrunning several government offices including the office of the Superintendent of Police, the district jail, the Treasury of Koraput district, killed 3 constables of the CRPF and a constable of the Orissa State Armed Police, looted 200 weapons including carbines and Self Loading Rifles and left without a single casualty.

West Bengal

Violence by the Naxals was at a low pitch as compared to the other States. This was because, West Bengal was one of the three states that enforced the Land Ceiling Acts legislated in the 1950s. In West Bengal, the land lords were called *Jotedars*, and the tenant farmers, *Bargadars*. Operation Barga under which the sharecroppers were registered and given permanent and inheritable rights on cultivation of their plots covered a total area of 11 lakh acres. Besides this 1.37 lakh acres of ceiling surplus and *benami* lands were acquired by the State Government and distributed among 25 lakh marginal and landless cultivators. The land reforms saw the emergence of a new class of farmers called the rural rich that weakened the social and political power of the landlords, who had hitherto dominated all the peasants in the rural areas.

The CPIM cadres have however after ruling for more than 25 years, become easygoing and probably slack in seeing that the lower castes and tribes regetting their due in some districts. It is not otherwise possible to explain the resurgence of the CPI Ml in Bankura, Purulia and Midnapore, where they began to recruit cadres and where a front organisation-Revolutionary Students Federation was formed in early 2004. They blamed the CPI M for following the diktats of a fascist centre. On 16 October, 2004, six personnel of the Eastern Frontier Rifles were killed in a land mine explosion in the Ormara forest of the West Midnapore district. A rally of seven extremist groups under the banner of Revolutionary Unity Committee, *Biplabi Sanhati Samity* was held in Calcutta on 15 December 2004. It was one of the biggest rallies since the sixties and was attended by old stalwarts Santosh Rana, Ashim Chatterjee, Azizul Haque.

What could be the reason for this revival of the extreme left? Obviously the CPI M had become stratified over the years. They had obviously not been able to see that all land with the upper classes had been taken away and redistributed to the landless poor farmers. Also the tribals in the forests had not been allowed to elect their own *Panchayats*? There is no doubt that there was a serious lacuna, hence the rally of the 15th December of 2004.

In 2010 and 2011, there was a clash between, the CPI M and the CPI Maoist in West Bengal. The surplus land that was with the *Jotedars* had been taken out from them by the District administration and distributed among the landless lower castes and tribes in several districts of West Bengal. However, towards the latter half of 2010, the CPI M Government of West Bengal decided to acquire agricultural land from small farmers for setting up a small car factory. These small farmers were the same landless farmers to whom the CPI M government had given land in the sixties and seventies after taking it out of the *Jotedars*. This was a regressive decision. The CPI Maoist immediately stepped in and took all these poor farmers under their fold. The situation created was a clash between the CPI M and the CPI Maoist. Very soon there were armed clashes between the CPI M and the CPI Maoist cadres! I am sure that the capitalist political parties of India must have had a good laugh.

The Naxalite Arsenal

In the formative stages, the Naxal cadres operated with guns stolen from the landlords. The story today is very different. The PWG, MCC and CPI Maoist have attacked Police Stations and armouries of the Police in several places and taken away large number of weapons on several occasions. The Ministry of Home Affairs has in an assessment stated that the CPI Maoist have 6500 regular weapons, including SLRs, rifles and carbines and AK47s, besides a large number of 12 bore guns. It is possible that the PWG had managed to get some AK 47 rifles from the LTTE. Many of the CPI ML, MCC, PWG, leaders had engineering degrees. The Andhra Pradesh Government had managed to unearth the manufacture of Rocket Launchers in a motor workshop in Vijayawada by one of these leaders. It is known that quite a number of small arms, grenades and explosives were collected from Nepal.

Links with insurgent groups in Northeast and Nepal

Links with the Maoists in Nepal was established many years ago. Links with the PLA of Manipur were established about a year or two ago. Sources in Manipur had informed this writer that the PLA of Manipur had developed links with the CPI Maoist in Jharkand and that some PLA cadres had been training Naxal cadres in Jharkand.

Analysis of the rise of the Naxal Movement

The CPI began work with the exploited scheduled class and tribe's way back in 1946. It is interesting that while all the upper castes in India trampled upon the rights of the lower castes and tribals it is only the CPI that first gave a hand to these exploited people located at the bottom of the caste hierarchy in India. The operations of the CPI in North Bengal and the Telengana area of the Nizam's kingdom have been narrated above.

When India got independence and the constitution was framed, the leaders who deliberated on the condition of the Indian peasantry framed the Ninth Schedule of the Constitution, that stated that India lived in its villages and there should be equitable distribution of cultivable land to all peasants. It is in consequence of the Ninth Schedule that every State in India legislated Land Reform laws in the first decade of our independence. Regrettably, except for three States, Jammu and Kashmir, West Bengal and Kerala, no State in India has implemented these laws on the ground. In a like manner, the Fifth Schedule of the Constitution was drafted with a view to protect the Tribals and their way of life so different from the caste Hindus, Muslims and Christians. As per the Fifth Schedule of the Constitution the Governor of a state was given the authority to administer the Scheduled areas of all the States except for the Northeastern States. The Scheduled areas are all the Reserve Forest areas of the State. The majority of the Adivasi tribals of India lived in these forest areas. The Governor was to administer these scheduled areas by appointing a Tribal Advisory Council from among the tribals living in that Scheduled area. Regrettably no Governor in the country since independence has ever exercised this right. After the Naxal trouble started and became serious, the Home Ministry set up a cell in the Home Ministry to study this problem and recommend solutions. It was probably based on the recommendations of this cell that the Government framed the Panchayat Extension to Scheduled Areas Act in 1996. This Act directs that in every forest area where tribals are living, they should have a Panchayat, who will decide how to administer their forest. For years, the *Baniya* or *Vaisya* trader had exploited the tribal who collected Forest Produce like tamarind, honey etc and brought it to the weekly village *haat* at the edge of the jungle for barter or sale. Here it was the Bania who bought his forest produce and sold him Kerosene oil, cloth, etc that the tribal did not have. The Banias have been generally cheating the tribal by taking several times the value of the goods that he bought from the tribal in exchange for the goods that he sold to the tribal. It is only when the CPI, or CPI M, or CPI ML or the CPI Maoist interceded that the bania behaved and gave the tribal the real value of his forest produce. It is seldom that a Collector or Deputy Commissioner ever supervised the barter in a village *haat* and ensured that the tribal got a fair deal. And as for cultivable land, this was always the birth-right of the upper caste and the lower caste dare not stake a claim to cultivable land. He was born slave on the lands of the upper caste forever and ever. When in the 1950's the Land Reform laws were enacted, no State except Kashmir ever even looked at it. In Kashmir, Sheikh Abdullah, the Chief Minister was the first to enforce the Land Reform laws legislated. This was done by him basically because most of the land lords were Hindus and the farm labour Muslims. Here also, many landlords, converted their paddy lands to Orchards and managed to bypass the Land Ceiling laws. In the rest of India, no State even looked at these laws. It was only when a coalition government was elected in West Bengal, in which the CPI M was a coalition partner that for the first time land ceiling was effected on the ground. The *Jotedars*, the land lords of West Bengal however did not give up so easily. They tried *benami* transfers of land to show that their holdings were less than the actual figure. It was at this point that a tribal young man filed a petition in a Magistrate's court that a piece of land allotted to him in enforcing the Land Ceiling law was not being handed over to him. He received a favourable order after the court heard the case. When he went to take over the piece of land, he was attacked by some goons of the landlord. This sparked an uprising by the tribals and other lower classes against the *Jotedars,* which spread to several parts of the State. This sparked off the Naxalbari Revolution.

The third State to enforce the Land Reform Laws was Kerala, when the CPI M was elected to power in the 1957 elections. It was E.M.S.Namboodripad, the Brahmin CPI M Chief Minister of Kerala who had these laws passed in the Assembly and also saw to it that the Land Ceiling was enforced. This Act was passed for the plains area of Kerala. It was a strong Act. It briefly stated that if a tenant farmer was a tenant in a piece of land for a period of 12 years, the ownership passed on to him without compensation. At a stroke, the tenant farmer found that he was the owner of the land that he was cultivating for his land owner for generations.

No other State looked at the Land Reform laws that they passed in their respective Legislatures. In view of the fact that the Telengana uprising took place in 1946, it was not surprising that the second agrarian revolution happened to be in Srikakulam district of Andhra Pradesh. After this the fire spread and engulfed Odisha, Bihar and Uttar Pradesh and took deep roots in Andhra Pradesh.

By not actively enforcing the deliberations of the Constitution and then not enforcing Land Reforms Acts legislated, the Governments of all these States have violated the Constitution and the Land Reforms Acts that each of these States passed in their Legislative Assemblies. Besides, looking at this primeval issue of land for each peasant, the States that refused to implement the Land Reforms that they themselves had passed in their respective Legislative Assemblies have thus committed a monstrous violation of India's Constitution. Further, looking at this in the background of the left parties having worked among the oppressed lower castes and tribals in North Bengal and the Telengana region of Andhra Pradesh from the early forties my conclusion is, that it is the dominant parties of India who ruled in all the States from 1947 for a decade, who created the space for the Left Extreme Groups to organise the Scheduled castes and the Scheduled tribes to fight the Government for their basic rights. Today, the Leftist groups have steadily gravitated to the left extreme and we have the CPI Maoist leading the revolt. All our think tanks scream that the Maoist is a threat to the Nation. Does anyone stop to ask who is responsible for this situation? Are not the so called democratic major political parties responsible for creating the space for the left extreme groups to lead the landless peasents in their quest for an equitable share in the ownership of cultivable land and for the Tribals of this country to live in the forests that have been their home for thousands of years and earn their livelihood from them?

A solution for the Naxalite Insurgency

One always hears in Seminars on India's Security concerns, when the issue of Naxalite insurgency is discussed, that development has not reached the interior and tribal areas and this is the cause of the insurgency. It is always stated that Communism is not to be tolerated in India and the Naxalite movement is to be crushed. So, what is to be done to solve this problem? The solutions are absurdly easy. The first step to be taken is that the Government must admit their mistake of not administering the Ninth Schedule of the Constitution and their Governors not invoking the Fifth Schedule of the Constitution and administering the Reserve Forests through the Tribal Advisory Councils.

Once the Government admits this, they should direct the States to implement the Land Ceiling Acts on the highest priority. The CRPF who are responsible for Counter insurgency operations in Naxal affected areas should be deployed in the segments that have been selected to enforce the Land Ceiling laws and ensure that the landlords who have been holding hundreds and thousands of acres of agricultural land in violation of the Land Reforms

Acts passed by the State Assemblies concerned surrender their surplus lands and that these are allotted to the landless peasants in the area. There will be attempts to revive groups like the Ranbir Sena in Bihar to disrupt the process of redistributing the cultivable land. Such attempts must be firmly dealt with declaring such groups as unlawful and ruthlessly disbanding them.

Once cultivable land is taken away from the upper class landlords and is distributed among the lower classes, they will begin to disassociate themselves from the Maoist organisers. The tribal cadres who have been trained as soldiers of the Maoists will then begin to desert their Maoist leaders. Announcements should be made over the radio that the tribal cadres who desert the Maoists will be returned to their tribal groups. They should be collected as they desert their Maoist organisers and granted amnesty.

For the forests, the CRPF should be deployed in a segment of the forest where about ten to twenty villages are situated. They should be so deployed that they are in sufficient strength in an arc to encompass the villages selected so that the Maoists who are entrenched in a deeper part of that forest are unable to interfere within the cordoned villages. Once this is done the District Magistrate should see that the Tribal Advisory Council for these ten/twenty villages are elected under the Panchayat Extension to Scheduled Areas Act and the Governor is informed. Then each forest village Panchayat will deliberate how the Minor Forest Produce will be collected. The Magistrate should now form a Forest Cooperative using educated tribals of that area who will buy the produce and market it through a Tribal Cooperative Marketing organisation to be set up at each district and then at the State level. The objective should be to cut out the insidious *bania* from this route.

If there are minerals in the concerned forest area, the Forest Panchayat should be directed to meet and decide how this mineral is to be extracted. Any MOU to be signed must be between the tribal Panchayat and the Company selected by the Tribal Panchayat to extract the minerals. The profits should go to the Panchayat and the villages comprising the Panchayat concerned. During this whole process, the task of the CRPF deployed around the forest enclave of ten forest villages will be to protect the ten villages from the Maoists and also the sharks in the industry who have been till now getting all the profits from the extraction of minerals from the mines inside the Scheduled areas.

Once this is implemented in a group of ten or twenty tribal villages, the process should be repeated in an adjacent group of tribal villages. Once a district is covered in this manner and the developments are covered by the press from the commencement, there would be an awakening among the tribals that the Government has finally woken up and are now treating the Tribals like they have been treating the upper classes. There will then be a clamour from all the tribal villages to implement the same plan in their areas. There will be a determined effort on the part of the Maoists to discredit the whole plan. This will have to be countered by a steady advance into all the tribal areas in a planned manner as per the modus operandi suggested above.

In this context we must look as to how the United States, Canada and Australia have treated the Red Indians and the Aborigines, whom they had fought and resettled in reservations denying them their hunting grounds. Today all these countries have apologised to the Red Indians and the Aborigines. Today these countries have passed laws which guarantees that if minerals or oil is discovered in the reservations of a Red Indian tribe or Aborigine group, it is the property of that Red Indian tribe or Aborigine group and it is for them to negotiate with a company to extract the minerals or oil and the profits go to that particular Red Indian tribe or Aboriginal group! If the United States and Australia could do this why cannot we do this?

2

India's Internal Security

EN Rammohan

Introduction

To understand India's internal security constraints we have to delve into history to make a dispassionate appreciation of the Indian Political, administrative and judicial system prevailing in the country.

India's main threats are from Pakistan and the Islamic fundamentalist groups nurtured and sponsored by that country. India also faces a threat from China because of the stance taken by us on the genocide in Tibet. We also have to take into account the political factors constraining our security template. Examined in the background of these factors it will be seen that the steps taken by us are woefully inadequate.

Historical Factors

Our main threat is from Pakistan and Islamic radicals in Pakistan and elsewhere, including in India, with bases in Saudi Arabia, Afghanistan, Bangladesh, and several Middle Eastern countries like Quatar, Abu Dhabi, Oman, Yemen, Kuwait who all shelter Islamic radicals. Islamic countries like Indonesia and Malaysia could also be involved. Above all this is the role of Saudi Arabia in financing the spread of Wahabi Islam all over the world and particularly in South and Southeast Asia.

India has a significant Muslim population. Unlike Christianity, Islam came to India with the sword. This is an inescapable fact and must always be kept in mind when we make any assessment of India's security. After

Muhammad established the religion of Islam in Arabia between 628 to 635 AD it spread fast to the north, east and the west. The first Muslim armies invaded India through Sind in the 8th century AD. They came across an idolatrous religion- Hinduism which was anathema to the new religion of Islam. The contrast and the incompatibility between the two religions has been the basic problem between the two communities since then. Islam spread throughout North India and a Caliphate was established in Delhi by the 14-15th century after the Mughal Empire consolidated its sway over the whole of North India and parts of Eastern Indiain what is now West Bengal and Bangladesh.

The British East India Company came trading to India in the 17th century, when the Mughals were in power at the caliphate in Delhi. Over the years the East India Company extended their stations all over India and by 1857 were administering several States directly and several kingdoms indirectly by allowing the local Rajas to rule under the guidance of a Political Officer and a local unit of the East India Company's troops. In 1857 there was an uprising mainly by the Muslim and Hindu soldiers of the East India Company's Army. The Sikhs did not join this Sepoy Mutiny and with their help the British troops quelled the mutiny. The British Government then took over the Government of India directly, shifting the capital to Delhi. One very significant change was effected by the British Government. When the East India Company spread its control, the language of administration was Urdu in most northern States. The British now changed this to English as the medium of administration. The British East India Company had allowed Christian Missionaries to work in India and many had set up schools where the medium of instruction was English. The majority of students who were sent to these schools were from Hindu families. When the medium of administration was changed from Urdu to English it was the Hindus who gained by getting recruited in all Government jobs. This led to a decline of the social standard of the Muslim population all over India. Instead of joining the mainstream the Muslims withdrew, led by their Religious schools like the Jamaat-e-Ulema-e Hind (JUH), founded at Deoband in 1869.

When the movement for Independence started in the first half of the 20th century, there was a lot of heart searching by the Muslim community. In an examination of the picture of undivided British India it will be seen that the portion that was bordering Afghanistan right upto the present Western Indian border except for the Southern portion of Sind was a majority Muslim area. The people of the Frontier Administered Tribal Areas (FATA) and the Northwest Frontier Province (NWFP) were majority if not totally Muslim areas. Punjab was divided equally between Muslims on the one side and Sikhs and Hindus on the other. Sind was a majority Hindu area. The Northern Territories were totally Shia Muslim, while in Kashmir, Jammu was a majority Hindu area, but Kashmir was a majority Muslim area. Ladakh to the east bordering Tibet was anthropologically Mongoloid and were majority Buddhist.

In the area that is now India and Bangladesh, there were areas like Uttar Pradesh, Bihar and East Bengal that had sizeable Mulsim populations, and small pockets like in Hyderabad, Bhopal and some Muslim Nawabships that had a majority of Muslims. In the run up to independence, the Muslim population set up a Muslim League in 1906 with its Head quarters at Dacca in East Bengal. It was the Muslim population of East Bengal that led the movement to establish this organisation.

As the independence movement began to gather momentum, there was a school of thought among a section of Muslims that India should not be divided. Maulana Maudoodi an Islamic scholar in undivided Punjab preached that at the height of the Muslim power in the world, there were three caliphates-the Caliphate of Sunni Islam in Baghdad, Iraq, the Caliphate of Shia Islam in Isfahan and the Caliphate of Sunni Islam in Mughal Delhi. He stated that these three Caliphates must not be changed. Maulana Maudoodi created a Muslim theocratic body called the Jamaat-e-Islami (JEI) in 1941 in undivided Punjab and stated that India cannot be partitioned.

Two other Islamic fundamentalist organizations originated in India, the Tablique Jamaat based in Nizamuddin New Delhi and the Ahle Hadith (AH) in Delhi which is in many respects very akin to the philosophy of the Wahabi sect in Saudi Arabia. These organisations are all very much against Sufism, a sect that came up because of the very rigid interpretations of Islam by the Ulema that took control of Islam after the death of its founder Muhammad. The TabliqueJamaat (TJ) has prospered in Pakistan and Bangladesh. The annual gathering of the faithful records more than a million people at Raiwind in Pakistan and Tongi in Bangladesh. In Pakistan the Military dictator Gen Zia-ul-Haq permitted the Tablique Jamaat to preach inside the Pakistan Defence Services cantonments that led to a strong Islamisation of the Defence forces there.

After independence, the Nizam of Hyderabad fought a mini war that lasted for seven months before Hyderabad could be absorbed into India. In Kashmir the Hindu Dogra ruler wanted to be independent and kept postponing a decision. His decision was precipitated by Cyril Radcliff's press conference where he stated that three tehsils of Gurudaspur district which was a Muslim majority district and hence slated to go to Pakistan would now be taken out and given to India. This act of treachery as far as Muhammad Ali Jinnah was concerned was attributed to Jawaharlal Nehru influencing Radcliffe through Lord Mountbatten. This triggered off an impromptu tribal invasion of Kashmir and a precipitate accession by the Maharaja of Kashmir to India and the first Indo Pakistan war of 1947-48. Kashmir has remained a festering sore since then. Unfortunately the governance of Kashmir has never been clean, though the development money given to Kashmir has not found its way back to Delhi as has happened in India's Northeast. Though most of the development money of Kashmir has been swiped by their own politicians and bureaucrats, the blame has gone to Delhi! Frankly, Kashmir has been spoilt by Delhi by treating it with kid gloves. One of the biggest mistakes that Delhi made was to neglect the hundred odd education centres that Sheikh Abdullah had started, to encourage the growth of Sufism. Today most of these institutions have either wasted away or been swallowed up by the Jamaat-e-Islami madrassas. Delhi had encouraged the Jamaat-e-Islami by funding them to pull down Sheikh Abdullah's supporters. This was akin to flirting with the devil! Over the years, instead of propping and supporting Sufi institutions in Kashmir, fundamentalist groups like the Jamaat-e-Islami and the Ahle Hadith have flourished in the Kashmir valley.

Muslim vote bank politics

The main political parties and many smaller groups in India have always treated the Muslims as a vote bank. This was started by the Congress and followed up by parties like the Samajwadi party in Uttar Pradesh, and even the Communist party of India Marxist in West Bengal. This partisan behaviour triggered off a reverse reaction in the Bharatiya Janata Party (BJP). One of the fallouts of this policy was the demolition of the Babri Masjid in Uttar Pradesh. For which both the Congress and the BJP were responsible. Years of pampering the Muslims in Gujarat led to a reverse reaction in 2001, when the BJP came to power in Gujarat and a veritable holocaust of a riot took place there. This led to a large number of young Muslim boys and even girls falling into the arms of a Muslim fundamentalist group called the Students Islamic Movement of India (SIMI). Dozens of young Guajarati Muslim boys were taken by SIMI indirectly to Pakistan via Mumbai, and Dubai, trained and returned by the same route in reverse. The sequel was the formation of the Indian Mujahideen and a series of bomb explosions and attacks by Pakistani Jehadi groups like the Lashkar-e-Taiba and the Jaish-e-Muhammad on Indian Institutions like the Indian Institute of Science Bangalore, the Red Fort in Delhi and culminating in an attack on the Indian Parliament.

The Introduction of Committed Bureaucracy

In the background of all this, one very important factor that is generally not mentioned is the development of a crucial factor in administration developed by the Congress party in 1975 during the emergency that was imposed on the country by Mrs. Indira Gandhi. This was the concept of Committed Bureaucracy. The first institution to fall after this pernicious system was introduced into the body politics of India was the Intelligence Bureau. It became a handmaiden of the Congress party and lost its professional edge in the process. It is the Intelligence Bureau that vets the candidates for the Congress party for the Lok Sabha and State elections in India since then. The result is a deep slide in the professional capability of the premier Intelligence Agency. This pernicious practice introduced by the Congress has been taken up by all political parties without exception. Regional parties and even the Communists in West Bengal and Kerala where they have ruled from time to time have followed this system. This has deeply affected the criminal justice system in all the States and in the Centre.

The sequel to the demolition of the Babri Masjid led to a reaction of Muslim dominated underground groups that had flourished in Mumbai in smuggling of drugs and other contraband along the sea route from the Middle

East and Pakistan into India. This group was patronised by the Congress government in Maharashtra and corruption in the Police force and Customs saw it flourish. When Babri Masjid was allowed to be demolished due to the Government's weakness, this Muslim led smuggling group brought in AK-47's, ammunition and explosives into Mumbai telling the Customs and the Police it was contraband and set off a large number of explosions in the city. Neither the Mumbai city Police, nor the Maharashtra Police nor the Intelligence Bureau had a clue to this. They were taken by surprise. This debacle can only be attributed to the politicisation of the Intelligence Bureau and the Police.

Regrettably no lessons have been learnt in this regard. The Intelligence Bureau continues to be under the control of the Party and its family in power. When 26/11 happened, we were again taken by surprise. This time the leader of the Muslim group who controlled the crime and smuggling in Mumbai who had fled Mumbai in 1992- Dawood Ibrahim was secure in Karachi protected by his Master, the Pakistan ISI.

In the background of these developments, how should we have reacted when 26/11 took place?

The first step should have been to delink the Intelligence Bureau and the Research and Analysis Wing from political interference. Unless this is done and professionalism is reintroduced into India's Intelligence Agencies, we will never be able to match the steps taken by the United States after 9/11, or indeed to carry put a professional review of our Intelligence machinery.

Let us take a look at what was the situation in India when the 26/11 commando strike by the Lashkar-e-Taiba took place. When the Kashmir insurgency took place it was entirely due to mishandling of the Kashmir situation by maligning the National Conference as being pro Pakistan, which was false. Prime Minister, Mrs Indira Gandhi did this because she felt that Farooq Abdullah, the heir apparent of the National Conference did not become an obedient follower. When the elections were held the Congress lost in Kashmir and over all in Jammu and Kashmir and Farooq took over as Chief Minister. She then made the mistake of destabilising Farooq by winning over his brother-in-law. She asked the then Governor of Jammu and Kashmir to buy some MLAs and destabilise Farooq. This, the then Governor Mr.

B.K.Nehru refused to do. Mrs Gandhi then transferred B.K. Nehru to Gujarat and posted a pliant lesson as Governor of J&K, who destabilised Farooq and appointed his brother-in-law as the Chief Minister. After she was killed in 1984, her son took over as Prime Minister. His advisors told him to befriend Farooq. When the elections were held with the Congress and the National Conference in a coalition, the people were naturally disgusted with the blatant rigging of the elections. A whole group of young men in Kashmir crossed over to Pakistan to ask help to be trained and armed to fight the Indian Government. What the Inter Services Intelligence (ISI) and the Pakistan Army had tried and failed from 1947 till 1988 was given to them on a platter.

It was shortly after a very violent insurgency had started in Kashmir that Babri Masjid happened, this time alienating the Muslims not only of Jammu and Kashmir but of the whole of India. The reaction to the demolition of Babri Masjid was the serial explosions in Mumbai organised by a gang of smugglers and illegal foreign exchange dealers, led by Dawood Ibrahim that had also by then established links with the Pakistan ISI. After setting up the serial bombs, Dawood Ibrahim left for Pakistan and has since then been continuing operations of recruiting volunteers for jihad in India, taking them to Pakistan via the Middle East, training them and bringing them back and organising bomb blasts, and raids in a series of violent unlawful incidents.

After the first retaliation against the Babri Masjid demolition, the Muslim fundamentalists regrouped. It was in Pakistan that the ISI seized the opportunity offered by the hurt Muslim community in India and began organising the fundamentalist groups like theLashkar-e-Taiba, the Harkat-ul-Jihad-e-Islami (HUJI). There followed a series of incidents in several parts of India. The incidents that were very bad were bombs that were set off in busy market places like the explosions in Sarojini Nagar market in New Delhi on a busy eveningthat killed and injured several innocent citizens. A few years later there was a similar serial explosion in Lajpat Nagar New Delhi. In between explosions of the same type took place in other cities of India like Hyderabad, Pune. Then there were even more daring attacks by trained Islamic insurgents on the Red Fort New Delhi, the Akshardam temple and finally the Lok Sabha.

One other significant development was the raising of a virulent Islamic fundamentalist group, the Indian Popular Front in far off Kerala. Islam came to Kerala long before it came to North India. The Arabs, long before Muhammad was born were sailing in their dhows along the western coast of India right down to Cape Comorin and from where they sailed to Malaya and Indonesia. The Arabs were then animist. When Islam was born, the Arabs brought the religion to Kerala and the rest of India's west coast. Since women did not generally sail with their men folk, the Moplah Muslim community was constituted by the Arabs inter marrying with the local women. Through the centuries the Hindus and Moplahs lived in amity. It is only after Khomeini's revolution in Iran in 1969 that a wave of fundamentalism swept India and South Asia right upto Southeast Asia. After the Babri Masjid demolition, this wave of fundamentalism gathered impetus and today you have Moplah Muslims from Kerala in the Lashkar-e Taiba, going to Kashmir and training there for jihad. In Kerala there was never any discrimination by the Hindus or Christians against the Muslims. Here at least the Muslims cannot cite a single example of communal behaviour by the Hindu or Christian community.

In this background our Intelligence Agencies in the Centre and the States should have completely revised their training syllabus. It will be necessary to make the Intelligence agencies both at the Centre and the States, get their cadres infiltrated into the Muslim fundamentalist groups to get information of developments in the different groups. This is not an easy task and has to be approached with thorough professional expertise. There are a hundred different ways to listen into the plans of the fundamentalist groups like the Indian Mujahideen or the Indian Popular Front or the Lashkar-e-Taiba or the HUJI. Similarly all the Indian Muslim fundamental organisations like the JUH, the JEI, the TJ, and the AH should be penetrated and any violent plans neutralised. This will have to be a continuous professional battle. All this is possible only if the Political parties become professional and do not make the Muslim community as a vote bank. Politically all religious groups should be treated as equals by all political parties.

The second field where intelligence can be gathered is in the field of electronic intelligence. I do not have to go into the detailed methodology here. The only point is that matters of privacy should not prevent electronic surveillance. When the Nation's security is at stake the State should come first.

If the political parties leave the Police and the Intelligence Agencies to function professionally and do not treat any religious group as a vote bank and indulge in propping them up, then the Nation's Security will not be at stake. Do we have the courage to go forward with this plan?

The Bangladesh Factor

East Bengal became a majority Muslim area after the Mughal Turks defeated the ruling Afghans who had dominated Delhi and North India for a couple of centuries. The major groups of Muslim rulers before the Mughal Turks came to power in Delhi were of Afghan origin. Pushed into Eastern India, the Afghan rulers established their control over Bengal. Muslim fundamentalist groups became active among this group of East Bengali Muslims and in the beginning of the 20th century; it was the Muslim leaders in East Bengal who started the Muslim League staking a claim for the creation of a Homeland for the Muslims.

When examining the history of Islam, we come across a watershed in the turn to fundamentalism in 1979, when Ayatollah Khomeini established religious control on Iran after overthrowing the Shah of Iran. This touched off a wave of fundamentalism across the Muslim world from Morocco in the west to Indonesia and the Philippines in the East. The next water shed was the invasion of Afghanistan a wholly Muslim country by the atheistic Communist Russia. If there is one thing that a Muslim abhors, it is a man who denies the existence of God. The rise of the Communist party in Afghanistan and the conversion of many Afghans to godless communists had already created great resentment among the true Muslims of Afghanistan. In Afghanistan, if there was one common factor among its people it was the call of the Muezzin to prayer. King Zahir Shah, the Prime Minister, the Chiefs of the Army and the Police, the Communist party chief and all their cadres, all without exception would go down on bended knees to do their *Namaaz* five times a day on the call of the Muezzin. When the Russians, impatient with their Afghan Communist leaders jumped the gun and sent their Communist Army rolling into Afghanistan, it was a simple recipe for disaster. No true Muslim could ever accept a godless army ruling them. The Muslim world was aroused and soon Muslim fundamentalist leaders like Abdullah Azam, Osama bin Laden and others had grouped in neighbouring Pakistan to organise a jihad against the ungodly Russian army that had rolled in through the Selang pass into Afghanistan. Volunteers to fight the ungodly Russians poured into Pakistan from Morocco in the west right across South Asia and South East Asia. Among the volunteers for the jihad were volunteers from Bangladesh. Years later when the Northern Territories were liberated from the control of the Taliban, an US citizen John Walker Lindh who had also come to Afghanistan to fight against the Russians was found in a prison camp in the Northern Territories. His interrogation revealed that there were three language groups in the jihadi training schools in Pakistan's North West Frontier Province. One was Arabic speaking and consisted of volunteers from the Middle East and Africa. The second was Urdu speaking. These were from Pakistan and also from Afghanistan. The third group was Bengali speaking and consisted of Muslim Bengalis from Bangladesh, the Rohingyas, a people of mixed Arakhan and Bangladesh origin, who spoke Bengali and came from Teknaf, the lowermost area of Bangladesh, south of Chittagong and Cox's Bazaar. The finance for all this training and sustenance of jihadi volunteers came from Saudi Arabia and other Muslim Emirates in the Middle East.

We are mainly concerned with the Bangladeshi and Rohingyas who went for training in Pakistan. Many fought against the Russian Army in Afghanistan, while many returned after a bout of fighting to Bangladesh. This resulted in the creation of a branch of the Harkat-ul-Jihad-e-Islami (Bangladesh) (HUJI-BD) and a branch of the Ahle Hadith in Bangladesh called the Ahle Hadith Andolan. By the time the Russians were defeated in Afghanistan, Bangladesh had become strongly Muslim fundamental. There was already a branch of the Jamaat-e-Islami in Bangladesh, who had played a notorious role in the Bangladesh Revolution against Pakistan by joining the Pakistan Army in their crackdown in early 1971 and killed hundreds of Bengali Hindus and Muslims who were part of the independence movement of the Awami League, the nationalist party of East Pakistan crusading for the creation of an independent East Pakistan to be known as Bangladesh.

This brings us to the main issue concerning the safety and security of India Vis a Vis Bangladesh. We have a 4000 odd kilometer long boundary with Bangladesh. Unfortunately, the line drawn by Cyril Radcliffe between India and East Pakistan was not a clear line as in the west between India and Pakistan. In the west except for two towns Attariand Munabao, which are located right on the border, there is not a single village on the zero line in the west. When the fencing was constructed on the western border in the early nineties, it was constructed a hundred yards behind the zero line. A track was made along the zero line for the BSF to patrol during the day. Where there were villages 100 yards behind the zero line the fence was constructed 100 yards from the border, leaving a gate for the villagers to come with their tractors for cultivation. The gates were opened at 0500 hours every day and closed and locked at 1800 or 1900 hrs depending on the time of last light. The western borders are thus effectively sealed and all petty smuggling has been reduced to zero. It is only occasionally that greed leads to attempts at smuggling heroin. This is done by mainly throwing heroin packets at prearranged designated places over the fence at night into the maize or wheat fields on the Indian side, to be collected later by the villagers involved in the smuggling.

In the East, there are more than a hundred villages situated right on the border, where in some cases the front doors of houses open into India, while the rear door opens into Bangladesh. There are also a number of towns situated right on the border, part of the town being in India and part in Bangladesh. Such towns are Hili in West Bengal, Agartala, Kamalpur and Khowai in Tripura, Karimganj in Assam. The Indo Bangladesh border is a scandal as smuggling is an open business between the poor people living on either side. In 1996-97 a proposal was submitted by the Border Security Force to the Home Ministry to resite the villages and towns located right on the zero line, a 100 yards behind the zero line and construct a strong double fence along the whole border between India and Bangladesh. Regrettably the Home Ministry has not taken this proposal seriously.

The most serious issue as a result of this negative policy is the easy access to fundamentalist elements of the JEI, the HUJI, the SIMI, the Indian Mujahideen and the AHA and related Islamic fundamentalists to slip into India place bombs in crowded towns and slip back into Bangladesh.

Bangladesh has become the sanctuary of Islamic fundamentalist elements operating in India. We have concrete examples of such movements. When the Harkutal Ansar (HUA) was sent into Kashmir to fight against the Indian Security forces in 1993, the Pakistan ISI sent the ideologue of the HUA Masood Azhar to Dacca, the capital of Bangladesh by plane, from where he sneaked into India through the porous border of Bangladesh and India, came to Calcutta and then by train and bus reached Kashmir, where he was captured by the Indian Army. There are a dozen recorded cases of such crossings by Islamic militants from Bangladesh into India and then back to Bangladesh across the porous borders of the Indo-Bangladesh borders.

We must take immediate steps to resite all the hundred odd villages located astride the Indo Bangladesh border. The villages must be resited a 100 yards behind the zero line and a strong fence as in the western border be constructed along the whole 4000 kilometres of the Indo Bangladesh border. Similarly, in towns like Agartala, Karimganj, Khowai and Kamalpur all the buildings astride the zero line must be demolished and reconstructed a 100 yards behind the zero line. There must be a clear belt of ground 100 yards from the zero line that should be only for movement of the BSF. A strong fence like in the west should be constructed parallel to the zero line a 100 yards behind, with gates for farmers if there is cultivable land ahead of the fence and till the zero line to be allowed for farming as in the western border.

Particularly after the 26/11 incident and the explosions in many of India's cities, it is certain that many of the mujahideen have slipped in from Bangladesh and slipped back after the crime. This is the first step that the Home Ministry should have taken after the 26/11 fiasco.

The Nepal border

There is a similar situation in the border between Nepal and India. There is no requirement of a passport for movement between India and Nepal and vice versa. It is however a known fact that the Pakistan ISI has a strong base in Nepal. It is a known route for Islamic fundamentalist cadres of different *Tanzeems* to go from Pakistan to Nepal and slip into India and after committing the crime of placing bombs slip back into Nepal and then move to Pakistan by plane. There are far too many recorded instances to be reproduced in this paper. We have yet not even thought of fencing the border. We have placed a force to guard this border only very recently. The same pattern of fencing as on the western border 100 yards from the zero line with gates must be adopted for this border too.

The Maritime Borders

Considering that the commando group of the Lashkar left Karachi by boat and sailed hugging the western coast of the Arabian Sea, hijacked an Indian boat midway and then sailed it for the rest of the distance to Mumbai, again hugging the coast and landed at Mumbaiin a fairly busy area without being intercepted was itself a shame. One should have expected that in view of the above, all the loose ends of coastal security would have been tied up by now and any attempt of the Laskar-e-Taiba repeating the effort could be ruled out. Far from it, recently two big ships one carrying cargo and another, oil grounded on the sandbanks off the coast of Mumbai city after drifting for a considerable period with neither the Coast Guards nor the Maharashtra coastal Police coming to know of this! One would have thought that after 26/11, the Coast Guard and the coastal Police units of the States on the Arabian Sea would have taken care of this issue.

It is imperative that every single fishing or any boat of whatever class must be registered with the coastal Police. There must be a system of checking each boat before it sails and after it beaches and there must be a system for surprise checks of such boats by patrolling craft of the coastal Police. The Coast Guards must operate fast medium craft for constant shore patrols covering about five kilometres from the base line of the Coast Guard Act, which is the shore line depending on the tide. This has obviously not been done.

It is also possible that trained LET or HUJI cadres could start from Cox's Bazaar and sailing up the coast of Bangladesh enter the Indian waters of West Bengal and enter the Calcutta port or Paradip or other ports on the Odisha Coast.

One other vulnerable area is the Kerala coast, which can be approached from a base in one of the vacant Laccadive Islands or the Maldives group. I am sure the Coast Guards have done their homework in this regard.

Internal checks of hotels, hostels and vulnerable institutions

After studying the video of the BBC on an interview of Headly, the agent who probably worked for both the ISI of Pakistan as well as the CIA, it is clear that he came to Mumbai, reconnoitered the targeted hotels and synagogue that was attacked in the commando raid of 26/11. My information obtained from confidential sources of security officers of Mumbai five star hotels is that some of the very commandos who came on the raid stayed in the targeted hotels during the preceding year and even cached arms, ammunition and grenades in the hotel that they used during the siege! I think we have a lot of rethinking to do regarding verification of guests in hotels and boarding houses before permitting their stay.

We also need to make much more use of CCTV cameras in public places to detect likely saboteurs from placing bombs.

3
Role of Air Power in Countering Maoist Insurgency

Gp Capt A K Agarwal

Since 1945, there have been more insurgencies than conventional wars.[1] The world has witnessed at least 89 insurgencies from 1945 to 2004.[2] The use of airpower in combating insurgencies is not a new idea. After the invention of the aero-plane, western powers found it to be a very useful weapon in subduing small insurgencies in their colonies fomented by rebellious tribesmen. The British used airpower to police their colonies and introduced a concept of 'Air Control' in policing them. It was found to be economically cheaper and effective.

Even in India, offensive airpower has been used in the past to put down insurgencies. On the 05 March 1966, the IAF was ordered to carry out strafing raids over Aizawl after Laldenga, the leader of the Mizo National Front (MNF) declared independence from the state of India. Twenty people

[1] Uttley Mathews. The Air Power Profession: Adaptions to Continuity and Change in the Strategic Environment. p-28. Article from: Airpower, Insurgency and the War on Terror, edited by Hayward Joel. RAF Centre for Air Power Studies.

[2] Gompert David C. and Gordon IV John Gordon IV.War by Other Means. Rand Corporation. p-439. http://www.rand.org/pubs/monographs/2008/RAND_MG595.2.pdf. Assessed on 20 Dec 2011.

[3] Minister's support for IAF bombing in Mizo Hills Criticised. The Assam Tribune 23 February 2010. http://www.assamtribune.com/scripts/detailsnew.asp?id=feb2310/oth05. Assessed on 25 March 2012.

were reportedly killed due to the airstrikes.[3] The air strikes in Mizoram are opined to have been instrumental in checkmating the Mizo insurgents and bringing the situation under control.[4] In the words of Major General DK Palit (Retd), "*5th March was the crucial day. At last, at 1130hrs came the air strike, IAF fighters strafing hostile positions all around the battalion area. The strafing was repeated in the afternoon… (6th March)… There was another air strike that day and that put paid to the investment. The hostiles melted away.*"[5] By using airpower offensively, the Indian government took a difficult political decision, indicating to the insurgents that their call for independence would not be accepted.

The on-going Maoist insurgency being witnessed by India, like all insurgencies has been born out of socio- economic reasons and poor governance. Hence, the solution is a political one and not solely a military one. Therefore, a comprehensive government strategy is a pre-requisite in defeating the Maoist insurgency. Unsuccessful counterinsurgency campaigns such as the Portuguese operation in Africa, the French in Algeria and the Rhodesian Republic, were characterised by a strategy that viewed the insurgency almost solely as a military operation and ignored the political and economic dimensions of the conflict.[6] The role of security and military forces in fighting any insurgency has to be in support of the larger comprehensive strategy consisting of political, social, economic and security aspects. Any successful counterinsurgent strategy must incorporate a three-pronged approach.[7] The government must immediately address the reason of popular unrest; it must identify and obliterate the underground political infrastructure of the insurgent, and must defeat the insurgent military forces.

All successful insurgencies had foreign support. Unsuccessful

---

[4] Sanjeev Miglani, Bombing Your Own People: The Use of Airpower in South East Asia. Afghan Journal 19 April 2010.http://blogs.reuters.com/afghanistan/2010/04/19/bombing-your-own-people-the-use-of-air-power-in-south-asia/. Assessed On 25 March 2012.

[5] Gen. (Retd) DK Palit, Sentinels of the North East: The Assam Rifles. Palit and Palit Delhi.p. 264.

[6] Corum S Johnson & Johnson R Wray, Air Power in Small Wars, Fighting Insurgents and Terrorists, University Press of Kansas.pp- 425 -426

[7] Drew Dennis .Insurgencies and Counterinsurgencies, http://www.au.af.mil/au/awc/awcgate/cadre/au-ari-cp-88-1.pdf.p-22. Assessed on 21 Nov 11.

insurgencies like the Malayan Emergency of 1948 failed due to lack of external support. This support is crucial for financing and more importantly arming the insurgents. At present, the Maoist insurgency is not overtly supported by any foreign country, though there are indications that they are in possession of Chinese arms. If the Maoists start getting support from an external agency, there are probabilities that the insurgency will spiral out of control. This insurgency must be nipped in the bud so as to ensure that the country is not plunged into a violent insurgency akin to the one Sri Lanka faced.

To address the issue of lack of development in Naxal affected areas, the government created the 'Naxal Management Division' under the Ministry of Home Affairs on 19 October 2006. This Division is mandated with effectively tackling the Naxal insurgency from both security and development angles. To ensure the success of various schemes and development in the affected areas, a pre-requisite would be to have a secure environment. The Maoists are making all efforts to sabotage these schemes and prevent the development of roads, power and telecommunications by violence and terror tactics, aiming to portray the ineffectiveness of the local governance. For example, Chhattisgarh, the state with the worst history of Naxal violence over the last decade, is finding it difficult to implement the Centre's road construction projects in areas affected by left wing extremism. Of the 44 road projects sanctioned in the state under the first phase of the Centre's plan, only three were completed by the end of 2011. The first plan was approved in February 2009. The State Government also opines that these projects can only be undertaken if a secure environment exists and the writ of law prevails.

A secure environment is a pre-requisite for enabling the government to address the various grievances of the population and ensure economic upliftment of the insurgency affected areas. The writ of the government and not the insurgents' must prevail if the state is to be successful in solving the problems of the people. Therein lies the importance of defeating the Maoists

---

[8] Om Shankar Jha, Combatting Left Wing Extremism is Police Training Lacking. Occasional Paper No 3 IDSA June 2009. p- 3.

in the jungles and bringing them to the negotiating table. The government must use all its resources in doing so and not just leave it to the para-military forces not adequately trained for the job.[8]

A common assumption is that counter-insurgencies are won or lost by the ground forces, who utilise aphilosophy of "minimum force" and win the "hearts and minds" of the people. The role of air power in such conflicts has been over-looked. As per a study conducted by the Rand Corporation titled 'Air Power in the New Counterinsurgency Era', *"the role of airpower is downplayed, taken for granted, or simply ignored and it (air power) is usually the last thing that most military professionals think of when the topic of counterinsurgency is discussed."*

There is no doubt that ground forces would be able to create a secure environment. However, if integrated with the use of airpower, the insurgency would be contained in a shorter period, with lesser loss of life and with saving of resources.

When the word airpower is used, 'offensive action' and the use of immense fire power is what comes to one's mind first. Airpower is not just about bombing and the use of direct force through the medium of air. There are many other aspects of airpower which make it invaluable to any counter insurgency operation. The proper application of the distinctive characteristics of air power — speed, ability to overcome physical barriers, range, flexibility, and psychological effect, when utilised in support of the ground forces can produce significant synergetic effects. Counterinsurgency operations are by nature joint with air and land power being interdependent.[9] Therefore, there is a role for airpower in counterinsurgency operations.

Offensive Action

Insurgencies do not lend themselves to the offensive roles of air power and the use of immense fire power. Insurgencies lack large transportation, communications, or military targets. In addition, the insurgent is difficult to identify. The possibility of collateral damage is high. Excessive force can be counterproductive as it could erode the support of the people, who are the

---

[9] Counterinsurgency, FM 3-24. Headquarters Department of the US Army, December 2006. p-E-1.

[10] Ibid. p-E-2.

centre of gravity of counterinsurgency operations.[10] In today's media savvy world, direct action from the air resulting in innocent casualties can be blown out of proportions by the media. No political party would accept such adverse publicity. At the same time, the unfavourable publicity would help the insurgent by providing him with a platform for adverse propaganda. This does not imply that offensive airpower should not be used at all.

Application of offensive air power is historically most effective when insurgents concentrate in large numbers. This situation provides readily identifiable targets for aerial attack. Taking a cue from their friends in Nepal, the Maoists have been adopting 'Swarming Attacks'.[11] When these attacks are analysed, data indicates that normally a force of 200 to 300 Maoists carry out attacks on police stations, villages or construction sites. In 2004, a thousand strong Maoist force attacked the District Headquarters at Koraput, Odisha. In another incident in 2006, 2500 Maoists besieged a village in Dandewade district of Chhattisgarh.[12] Such large concentrations of Maoists definitely offer an identifiable target from the air. Limited utilisation of offensive airpower would have been helpful in repelling the insurgents, without the fear of collateral damage and injury to innocent bystanders.

Pre-planned Close Air Support is one of the most effective ways of applying airpower offensively. When Close Air Support is dovetailed into the ground operations, it has the advantage of being fully integrated. The area of interest is known in advance, target - weapon matching can be carried out and air power assets can be planned to respond to numerous contingencies. Detailed planning can ensure effectiveness with minimum collateral damage.

Nine helicopters, of which six belong to the Indian Air Force are in use for counterinsurgency operations against Maoists. The Cabinet Committee on Security headed by the Prime Minister has cleared the use of these

---

[11] Ajai Sahani. Maoists: Creeping Malignancy. *South Asia Intelligence Review*. Weekly Assessments & Briefings, Volume 5, No. 51, July 2, 2007. http://www.satp.org/ satporgtp/sair/Archives/5_51.htm#assessment1. Assessed on 28 March 2012.

[12] http://www.satp.org/satporgtp/countries/india/maoist/data_sheets/militiaattack.htm. Assessed on 28 March 2012.SalwaJudam is local a militia force in Chhattisgarh, which was aimed at countering the naxalite violence in the region. In 2011, the Supreme Court of India declared it illegal and it has since been disbanded.

[13] *The Telegraph*. 02 October 2009

helicopters for casualty evacuation and troop mobility. Helicopters have not been permitted to be used in the offensive role. In two incidents in the past, helicopters were attacked by the Maoists with AK-47 machine guns while coming in for landing.[13] A number of such incidents which may not have been reported by the media must have occurred. Intelligence inputs have been received saying that the Maoists are planning to shoot down helicopters carrying security personnel.[14] The Maoists are equipped with advance assault rifles and explosives and have the capability to carry out such attacks. In September 2009, a book titled 'Guerrilla Air Defence: Anti-Aircraft Weapons and Techniques for Guerrilla Forces' was recovered from them.[15] After attacks on the IAF helicopters, Rules permit the IAF to fire back, albeit only in self-defence. It is but a matter of time when the Maoists will be successful in shooting down a helicopter involved in anti-Maoist operations. This will be a political victory for the Maoist and an embarrassment for the government. It brings to mind a question as to why should the IAF only shoot back after they are hit. What is the harm in sanitising the landing area by offensive fire from the air prior to the helicopter sitting down? The IAF could also have another helicopter hovering in perch, looking out for any hostile activity from the ground and answering it befittingly with machine gun fire. During the Algerian Insurgency, the French mastered the art of clearing the landing ground of insurgents by offensive action and timing the arrival of the helicopters just after such actions.

It is time that the government adopted a more offensive approach towards fighting the Maoist insurgency, described by the PM of India as one of the biggest security threats to the country. Offensive action by helicopters, when pre-planned, could save the lives of many security personnel involved in counterinsurgency operations. Such operations could be carried out while raiding known Maoist training camps. In March 2010, a Maoist training camp was attacked by the security forces. Helicopters were used for transporting the troops. A huge quantity of arms and ammunition and explosives were recovered. However, most of the Maoists were able to escape. This operation is a classic case where helicopters

---

[14] *The Pioneer.* 08 October 2011.
[15] DNA 12 April 2010.

could have been employed more offensively, without the fear of collateral damage to innocent civilians. Helicopters could have been used to neutralise the camp from the air and thereafter troops inducted for mopping up operations.

Support Roles

Troop Mobility. Rough terrain and poor surface connectivity can be serious impediments to counter insurgency operations while they are advantageous to the insurgents. The Maoists follow guerrilla tactics, taking the initiative to attack security forces at their place of choice and time. They ambush patrolling security forces in isolated areas, and disappear before reinforcements arrive. They frequently mine roads and are successful in blowing up vehicles used by the security forces. Airpower can help overcome these impediments.

Counterinsurgency operations in Chhattisgarh and Odisha are being conducted in inhospitable terrain laced with thick jungles and at times mountainous obstacles. The versatility of the helicopter in being able to operate in any kind of terrain can be exploited to counter Maoist insurgency in inhospitable terrain. Its ability of vertical landing and take off and hover are ideally suited to the jungle terrain. Troops are required to march through thick jungles to reach insurgent infested areas. The operational use of helicopters can be made for transporting troops directly into the area of interest, ensuring that the troops reach fresh, fully rationed, alert for battle and most importantly with complete surprise.

Casualty Evacuation. The helicopter is ideally suited for Casualty Evacuation (Casevac) role. With its ability to land in small clearings and evacuate battle casualties or hover to winch up injured soldiers where no suitable landing area exists, it is a great morale booster to the ground forces. To any wounded soldier, the knowledge that a smooth ride in a helicopter to hospital is assured instead of a journey through the jungles or tough terrain on a stretcher will give them tremendous confidence about their survivability and uplift their morale. A corollary to this is that such injuries would not divert manpower towards tending to the injured and as a result not hamper operations.

Intelligence, Surveillance and Reconnaissance (ISR). A major factor for the police and security forces being unable to suppress Maoist insurgency is the lack of reliable information and intelligence. The security forces are finding it difficult to monitor the activities of the Maoists through HUMINT and carry out intelligence based operations.[16] Even elite CoBRA battalions are devoid of intelligence flow from the ground level[17] the CRPF has only eight intelligence operatives per battalion, a very insignificant figure considering the task requirement.[18] The lack of intelligence is evident from what the Home Minister of India had to say while inaugurating the first-ever intelligence training school for Central Reserve Police Force (CRPF) officers and personnel, *"The CRPF, a key force in anti-Naxal operations, will have to acquire an intelligence-based strategy to combat Maoists who have organised themselves as a regular fighting army."*[19]

Obtaining intelligence is very important to the success of counterinsurgency operations. Airpower provides a very efficient intelligence collection method. The ability of airpower to provide opportune, wide area surveillance and reconnaissance in counterinsurgency operations remains vital to the chances of their success. Modern technology has enabled aircraft to monitor large areas from the air. With the advent of Unmanned Air Vehicles (UAVs), airborne surveillance has become more effective. Modern UAV platforms have the ability to stay airborne for long durations. They are equipped with state of the art surveillance equipment that has the capability to provide real time and clear imagery of large areas of remote ground stations. These platforms can operate over areas of interest unobtrusively and persistently. Thus they are ideally suited in the ISR role for counterinsurgency

---

[16] Mohan Vishwa. Centre looking into MPVs' vulnerability in anti-Naxal war. The Times of India 24 January 2012. http://articles.timesofindia.indiatimes.com/2012-01-24/india/30658663_1_mpvs-naxal-violence-naxal-problem.Assessed on 24 March 2012.

[17] Sharma Rajnish. CoBRA Not Able To Bight Naxals. The Asian Age, 27 February 2012. http://www.asianage.com/india/mha-worried-over-futile-cobra-ops-838. Assessed on 27 March 2012.

[18] Bring Intl Based Approach to Combat Maoist: PC to CRPF. Deccan Herald 08 February 2012. http://www.deccanherald.com/content/225543/bring-intel-based-approach-combat.html. Assessed on 27 March 2012.

[19] Ibid.

[20] Brook Tom Vanden. Air Force Seeks More Fighter Drones.USA Today.06 March 2008. http://www.usatoday.com/news/washington/2008-03-05-Reapers_N.htm. Assessed on 23 January 2012.

operations. In the words of Loren Thompson, a military analyst at the Lexington Institute in USA, *"Unmanned vehicles present a whole new dimension to detecting and destroying of terrorists' cells, it's almost like having your own little satellite over a terrorist cell."*[20] With the ability to provide 24 hour surveillance, ISR capabilities are able to establish a pattern of life more effectively than inputs from ground based sources, as experienced by American forces in Iraq and Afghanistan.[21] Continuous airborne surveillance of insurgency infested areas, when combined with other sources of intelligence, increases the possibility and probability for security forces to take the initiative from the insurgents. UAVs can support paramilitary patrols by flying ahead to detect possible threats. Once detected, the ground force can manoeuvre around the threat or call in air or other fire support against it. Airborne surveillance can also monitor the likely escape routes that the insurgents will take and guide the security forces accordingly.

Intelligence gathered by aerial platforms can give you a great amount of data. It can observe the pattern of life and discern any changes in such routine patterns. However, it cannot give answers to the reasons for the changes. Counterinsurgency operations are dependent on effective intelligence, which can be analysed only by individuals who are familiar with the ground situation and also have sufficient operational experience in fighting the insurgency. Intelligence gathered through air assets must be quickly routed for timely analysis. The availability of actionable intelligence to the field is hastened by the combination of gathering data through aerial and HUMINT assets and its analysis by experienced individuals.

Psychological Effect. In the fight against an insurgency, in order to reduce or destroy the insurgents' military ability to wage the insurgency, there will be two effects -the physical and the psychological. The physical aspects are the discernible ones like physical destruction of insurgents, their equipment and training camps and other viable targets. However, the psychological aspects are the more indiscernible ones in which targeting the 'hearts and

---

[21] Mulrine Anna. A Look Inside the Air Force's Control Center for Iraq and Afghanistan. US News. 29 May 2008. http://www.usnews.com/news/world/articles/2008/05/29/a-look-inside-the-air-forces-control-center-for-iraq-and-afghanistan?page=2. Assessed on 23 January 2012.This article describes the operations at an Air Force Control Centre and how UAVs are being used effectively in identifying and tracking insurgent groups.

minds' instead of winning them is the main concern. The desired outcome of the psychological campaign is to target the insurgent's mind and render his forces reluctant or unwilling to continue with the insurgency. Degradation or destruction of the insurgents' resolve to continue fighting has a similar effect on his combat capability as actually degrading or destroying his perceivable assets. Hitting the insurgents' critical vulnerabilities for both physical and psychological effect can produce a synergistic outcome on the insurgents' capacity to continue waging the insurgency. It must be noted that these psychological effects of airpower will only be visible when a decision has been taken to use airpower offensively. In a study done by the Rand Corporation, *"in the conflict situation in which the enemy troops were not subject to sustained, effective attacks, their resistance did not collapse and they did not surrender and desert en masse."*[22]

The psychological effects of offensive operations on the local population, which is detrimental to counterinsurgency operations must be minimised. Civilian casualties must be avoided at all cost, as the innocent civil population is the centre of gravity of any counterinsurgency campaign. Their support has to be won over and not lost by collateral damage from aerial attack. This would depict the government in poor light for using excessive force against innocent civilians.

Other than creating a feeling of despondency and lowering the morale of the insurgent, airpower can be used gainfully in creating a feeling of security in the minds of the local population and portraying the security forces as competent and efficient force with humane face. Airpower can be integrated into 'Winning the Hearts and Minds' campaign. A very effective method of winning the hearts and minds of the insurgency effected local population and their support in the fight against insurgency, is by employing air transport to airlift or drop food and medical supplies to citizens living in isolated areas. Another important role would be to bring governance to the doorstep of remote villages not well connected by road, by conveying civil

---

[22] Hosmer T Stephen. Psychological Effects of US Air Operations in Four Wars 1941-1991. Rand Corporation. p-xxiv.

government functionaries to oversee local administration and development.

Air Power Helps in Reducing Force Levels. With the judicious application of airpower in the ISR, troop mobility, logistic supply, casualty evacuation and offensive support roles, the force level can be reduced to a great extent.[23] As seen in past insurgencies, counterinsurgent to insurgent force ratios can vary from 10 as in Algeria to 50 as in Jammu and Kashmir.[24] During the Malay Emergency,where the force ratio was 12,[25] it was estimated that without the use of helicopters, four times the number of ground troops would have been required to fight the insurgency.[26]

Counterinsurgency operations are manpower intensive. Airpower when used to transport troops and in other administrative duties, provides numerous advantages.

(a) Troop movement by air enables the ground forces to avoid moving by roads which are vulnerable to being mined or the troops ambushed. By moving counterinsurgency forces by air, it does away with the requirement of protecting convoys with a significant number of troops. This in turn frees security forces from such secondary duties and permits them to be deployed in counterinsurgency operations – resulting in an overall reduction of forces.

(b) Transporting troops by air denies the insurgent with a lucrative target and an opportunity for adverse propaganda for the government.

(c) Airborne logistic supply hastens resupply of troops in the field, enabling them to move lighter resulting in more incessant ground

---

[23] Op.cit. Corum.p-435

[24] Rabasa Angel, Warner Lesley Anne, Chalk Peter, Khilko Ivan and ShuklaParaag. Money in the Bank- Lessons Learnt from Past Counterinsurgency Operations. Rand Corporation. p-xiv. http://www.rand.org/pubs/occasional_papers/2007/RAND_OP-185.pdf. Assessed on 04 January 2012.

[25] Goode Steven M. A Historical Basis for Force Requirements in Counterinsurgency.p-51. http://www.carlisle.army.mil/usawc/parameters/Articles/09winter/goode.pdf. Assessed on 11 January 2012.

[26] Peterson, Reinhardt and Conger.Op.cit. p- 72.

operations.

(d) By doing away with resupplying the troops by road, the chances
     of losing the supplies to insurgent ambushes also reduce,
     resulting in reducing the amount of redundant supplies and man
     hours that must be used for pushing supplies into the system
     catering for losses. This also acts to the disadvantage of the
     insurgent who may depend upon captured government logistic
     supplies to sustain him. This is evident from the incident in
     Chintalnar in Chhattisgarh where the routine bus run carrying
     rations for the CRPF camp was hijacked by the Maoists,
     depriving the troops their daily ration and aiding in sustaining
     the Maoists.[27]

Role of the Media. With the proliferation of TV news channels and culture
of 'Breaking News', public opinion is very easily formed depending on how
the news is projected to the audience. If air power is to be used in fighting
an insurgency in a democratic state, especially offensive airpower, the people
must be convinced that excessive force is not being used, nor are civilians
being attacked indiscriminately. The media, which is known to be very
responsible in reporting matters of national security,has to be taken into
confidence and explained the requirements and advantages of using airpower
in all its roles.

Conclusion

The wars of the twenty first century are going to be insurgencies and other
low intensity conflicts. Police action may not be successful in quelling these
conflicts and terming them as internal law and order problems of the state
may not be a correct analysis of the situation. 223 Districts across 20 states
experience Maoist activity as compared to 20 Districts in the state of J&K.[28]
Naxalite related fatalities are more as compared to the combined number of

---

[27] PandeyBrijesh. Hard Battles Hard Lives.Tehelka Magazine, Vol. 7, No. 29, July 24,
2010. http://www.tehelka.com/story_main46.asp?filename=Ne240710CoverStory.asp.
Assessed on 25 March 2012.

[28] India Assessment 2011. www.satp.org/satporgtp/countries/india/index.html. Assessed
on 02 April 2012.

[29] Ibid.

all other terrorist and insurgent movements in the country.[29] The government needs to pull out all stops and review its strategy against this insurgency. In suppressing the insurgency in Mizoram, the Government of India used airpower as a last resort. Before the country is faced with a similar situation, the government must use all the means at its disposal, which include airpower in both the offensive and support roles.

Airpower will not be able to eliminate the requirement of having ground forces deployed in counterinsurgency operations. But airpower will definitely enhance the ground forces ability to gather intelligence and locate the insurgents, increase their mobility and sustainability, extend their reach and fire power, in other words act as a force multiplier. This opens up a number of courses of action which can be employed to either neutralise or capture the insurgents. Airpower enables the ground commander to commit a smaller force to achieve the same goals.

4

India's Internal Security Architecture: Learning from US Homeland Security

Brigadier Amrit Pal Singh

The terror attacks on September 11, 2001, in the United States (US) and on November 26, 2008, in Mumbai, India, were the catastrophic events that became catalysts for security reform in both nations. A whole new approach towards integration of detection and response to terror began evolving in the US immediately thereafter. India set itself on a path to reform after public outcry against inefficient detection and response to the urban siege in Mumbai. The Indian efforts to reform the Internal Security (IS) mechanism have modeled themselves on the transformation that Homeland Security has undergone in America. This special report is an attempt to compare the path that reforms in the US have taken starting with the recommendations by the National Commission on Terrorist Attacks upon The United States (9/11 Commission) to the IS reforms being attempted in India.

This report studies the two mechanisms by starting with the approaches taken by the US and India in the immediate aftermath of 9/11 and 26/11 respectively and looks at the introspection both countries have carried out and how reforms started. The laws enacted to strengthen the security environment of India and those like the USA PATRIOT Act and The Intelligence Reform and Prevention of Terrorism Act (2004) of the US are discussed with a view to evaluate their adequacy. Intelligence mechanisms and information sharing by the systems in both countries is reviewed to analyze the changes proposed in India. The centrality of sound intelligence to effectively countering terror has been recognized by policy makers in both countries. The reorganization and repositioning of intelligence agencies in India has yet to take place, as they have in America, due to reasons like turf guarding and dynamics of the various power centers that exist in India. These obstacles to reform must come down. With strong relations between India and the United States, India can take the lessons learned in the US so far and incorporate those lessons. This iterative learning process will allow India to advance its reforms significantly.

The 9/11 Commission's Recommendations

The 9/11 Commission underscored not only the enormous challenges to create the technical infrastructure to more effectively and efficiently share intelligence, but also to rethink the web of "need to know" and other security requirements that frustrate sharing. The 9/11 Commission made six broad proposals:

- Creation of the position of Director of National Intelligence (DNI), with real authority over the budgets of the 15 US intelligence agencies.

- Institute a National Counterterrorism Center (NCTC) reporting to the DNI, responsible for joint operational planning and joint intelligence.

- Establish national intelligence centers, organized around discrete issues on the model of NCTC, under the authority of the DNI.

- Make the Central Intelligence Agency (CIA) Director a position separate from the DNI and make the director primarily responsible for building a better espionage capacity for the nation.

- Set focal points for oversight in both the House and the Senate, for both intelligence and homeland security, in place of the 88 committees and subcommittees of Congress.

- Rethink the web of "need to know" and other security procedures that frustrate not just sharing intelligence but also intelligence work as a whole.

The 9/11 Commission specifically opted against creating a separate domestic intelligence service, on the model of the British MI5 instead, the Federal Bureau of Investigation (FBI) should move forward with changing its mission from pure law enforcement to terrorism prevention and building a Directorate of Intelligence within the existing FBI.

The most far-reaching recommendation, however, was the commission's proposal to achieve coordination like the military in separating the "organize, train, and equip" functions from the actual deployment of intelligence personnel. The existing agencies—CIA, FBI, Defence Intelligence Agency (DIA), and National Security Agency (NSA)—would, like the military services, be responsible for building the intelligence forces. Those forces, however, would be used by the new national intelligence centers, which would be shaped by issue or function, not as now by organization or collection source.

Specifically, the NCTC would be the command center in the war on terrorism, responsible for intelligence analysis and planning operations; the CIA and other agencies would provide the analysts and other personnel and would conduct the required operations. Issue-oriented centers have existed in the intelligence community since the mid-1980s. In form, these centers, like the preexisting Counterterrorism Center (CTC), worked for the DCI; however, in reality, the CIA dominated these centers. The Intelligence Reform and Prevention of Terrorism Act of 2004 would move them to the DNI and, in principle, make them more central as focal points for intelligence and operations.[1]

Despite the requirement being felt for many years for a central coordinator of Intelligence in the country, the main reason a post like the DNI was not created was that none of the most critical officials wanted the change. DCIs have not wanted to trade their CIA assets for the uncertain prospects of being an intelligence overlord. The growing importance of the three big technical collectors of intelligence with the Department of Defence (DoD) increased the defence establishment's opposition to giving a DNI

---

[1] Gregory F. Treverton, 'The Next Steps in Reshaping Intelligence', RAND Corporation occasional paper, p-4

control. It took the shock of September 11 and the pull of the victims' families, plus the artful connecting by the 9/11 Commission of that failure with the need for a DNI, plus continued lobbying by the commission members to make the December 2004 bill passed by the President a reality.[2]

Proposed architecture in India

A year after the 11/26 attack in Mumbai, the Home Minister (HM) in December 2009 announced a set of radical changes and repositioning when outlining architecture for Internal Security in India. He suggested restructuring of the Ministry of Home Affairs (MHA) with an aim to make the HM solely responsible for matters relating to security. Subjects not directly related to internal security should be dealt with by a separate ministry or should be brought under a separate department in the MHA and dealt with by a Minister, more or less independently, without referring every issue to the HM.

Setting up of NATGRID. Databases that contain vital information and intelligence are to be networked, as each database currently stands alone and various such databases lack interoperability. As a result, crucial information that rests in one database is not available to another agency. In order to remedy the deficiency, the Central Government has decided to set up NATGRID. Under NATGRID, 21 sets of databases will be networked to achieve quick, seamless and secure access to desired information for intelligence/enforcement agencies. This project is likely to be completed in 18 – 24 months.

National Counter Terrorism Center (NCTC). Under the new proposal, India was to set up the NCTC by the end of 2010 however, there are inevitable delays and, once set up, the center is to have the broad mandate to deal with all kinds of terrorist violence, directed against the country and its people. This will include preventing a terrorist attack, containing a terrorist attack should one take place, and responding to a terrorist attack by inflicting pain upon the perpetrators.

Repositioning of Intelligence Bodies. The positioning of Research and

---

[2] Ibid, p-9.

Analysis Wing (R&AW), Aviation Research Centre (ARC) and Central Bureau of Intelligence (CBI) would be re-examined to place them under the oversight of NCTC to the extent that they deal with terrorism. The intelligence agencies of the Ministry of Defence and the Ministry of Finance would continue to remain under the respective Ministry, but their representatives would have to be deputed mandatorily to the NCTC.

Policing and Criminal Tracking. To achieve connectivity, the Central Government proposed implementing an ambitious scheme called Crime and Criminal Tracking Network System (CCTNS). The goals of the system are to facilitate collection, storage, retrieval, analysis, transfer and sharing of data and information at the police station and between the police station and the State Headquarters and the Central Police Organizations. The police force is to be modernized with more police stations and, at the police station level, more constables, some of whom are exclusively for gathering intelligence. A system of community policing, a toll-free service, and a network to store, retrieve and access data relating to crimes and criminals is proposed.

Indian Security Environment

Neighbourhood

Almost all of India's neighbours can be broadly described as "troubled states" and there is always the potential danger of spillover effects arising from unstable conditions of the "neighbourhood." The cauldron of terror in Pakistan, Maoist participation in Nepal's government, the ethnic problem in Sri Lanka, the increasing menace of smuggling and drug trafficking, and conflicts in Pakistan and Bangladesh will have important implications for India. The involvement of external forces in aiding and abetting India's organized crime and mafia groups, encouraging trans-border illegal migration, money laundering operations, gun-running and drug trafficking, apart from fomenting criminal and subversive activities, as well as religious and ethnic conflict cannot be understated. Enormous funds generated by transnational crime networks and narco-terror are likely to be used to spread Islamic fundamentalism and organize ethnic conflict and other violent incidents all over the country.

The internal security system in India is fragmented with numerous examples of how the lack of a single institution in charge of the country's first ring of defence costs the system in terms of efficiency. An example of the divisions is the coastal defence, which was penetrated during the 11/26 attacks. It is divided between three different agencies: the State coastal police, the Coast Guard and the Navy. The number of vessels authorized to be in deep waters is difficult to ascertain as records of movements of vessels are held by a different set of agencies: customs, the Directorate of Fisheries of the state concerned and the Mumbai-headquartered Directorate of Shipping. Border control is particularly important to India on its porous borders with countries that are home to elements hostile to the country and a long coastline. Border sealing is rendered ineffective also due to the politician-crime nexus that thrives on smuggling.

Politics of Security

The other aspect that limits the Indian government's role in strengthening internal security is its quasi-federal Constitution. Under the Indian Constitution, "public order" and "police" are under the jurisdiction of the states and not the central government. Consequently, individual states have powers under Article 246 to make laws and take all necessary executive action to maintain internal security. The central government's responsibility under Article 355 of the Constitution prescribes that it is the duty of the union to protect the states against external aggression and internal disturbances and to ensure that every state is governed in accordance with Constitution.

Under Article 356, Presidential rule can be established until constitutional governance can be restored. Article 352 of the Constitution provides for the enforcement of emergency rule if a situation warrants or if there is imminent danger to the security of India such as threat of war or armed rebellion. This possibility leads to a situation of apprehension of a political party or coalition governing a state different from the ruling party or coalition at the center. The state government in such states is extremely sensitive to central intervention, even in cases of severe internal conflicts, be it terrorism or insurgency.

The frequent misuse of central government power in the past and the regular abuse of central intelligence agencies have further vitiated center-state relations. The resultant mistrust between the central and state governments make it increasingly difficult to devise and implement suitable laws to deal with the challenges to the country's internal security. Any talk of creating an adequately stringent law applicable to the whole country, which would effectively deal with terrorist offences, cyber crimes and the fast-growing areas of organized crime that pose a grave threat to national security, results in huge controversies. Partisan politics is hampering the creation of a federal crime agency that could deal with serious offences committed by criminal networks whose activities may spread across states and the entire country and cross over to foreign lands.

In the aftermath of the Mumbai attack the National Investigation Agency was set up and a decision has been taken to deploy the National Security Guard (NSG) in the four metros immediately and in the long run to all state capitals in the country. The parliament passed in record time the Unlawful Activities (Prevention) Amendment Act 2008 which would inter alia allow the detention of terror suspects for up to 180 days. These steps are important, but they do not substantially enhance the Indian capability to counter terror. They qualify as interim measures allowing time for an honest re-appraisal of the existing counter-terror mechanisms. Internal security can no longer be considered a part-time job of the HM (along with Centre-state relations and minority issues).

Two major policy initiatives have been recommended by the HM: exclusive responsibility of political oversight over IS machinery by the HM and limited executive role in IS management by the National Security Advisor (NSA). The HM traditionally had under his administrative and operational control the Intelligence Bureau and the various central police organizations or Para-military forces. He also had the responsibility for guiding and coordinating the work of the state police forces.

This clear line of responsibility got increasingly diluted or blurred due to various reasons such as the creation of new agencies for security-related duties (the Special Protection Group (SPG) for the security of the incumbent and past prime ministers and their families and the National Security Guards (NSG) as a special intervention force against terrorism). The SPG and the

NSG were as a result of political events made to work under the political oversight of the prime minister and the operational oversight of the cabinet secretary.[3]

Terrorism, with its international dimensions has necessitated co-operation with the counter-terrorism and homeland security agencies of other countries. Diplomacy in turn assumes an important role in counter-terrorism particularly against state sponsors of terrorism. The US created a counter-terrorism division in the State Department to deal with these international and diplomatic dimensions. It continues to function even after the creation of DHS. India gave the international and diplomatic dimension greater importance gradually and a number of joint counter-terrorism working groups with different countries came into existence and joint counter-terrorism exercises were organized with interested countries. While the responsibility for the co-ordination of the international and diplomatic dimensions was given to the Ministry of External Affairs, the MoD exercised the co-ordination responsibilities in respect of joint counter-terrorism exercises.

With terrorist organizations acquiring or attempting to acquire specialized capabilities for catastrophic terrorism, the need for India to acquire specialized counter-capabilities increased. To meet these needs, the role of the MoD, the armed forces and the various science and technology institutions were enhanced. The problems in India arise from the fact that terrorism has increasingly assumed new dimensions and new frontiers. Yet, no attempt has been made to work out a comprehensive approach to deal with terrorism in its classical form, terrorism in its post-9/11 form and likely future forms of terrorism. The threat posed by terrorism continues to evolve, whereas, in India, concepts to deal with it have not kept pace with the threat.

It is apparent to many observers that the executive role has to be that of the HM, with the NSA taking an active role in evolving concepts. The NSA is better able to develop a comprehensive inter- departmental governmental approach to internal security and counter terrorism. The NSA also would also be the right entity for coordinating and supervising the evolving machinery to facilitate India taking advantage of the growing international

---

[3] B.Raman, 'Revamping of the internal security machinery', http://intellibriefs. blogspot.com/2010/02/revamping-of-internal-security.html.

co-operation against terrorism. The HM, or a new ministry for internal security, is best suited to handle the nuts and bolts of internal security activities on a day-to-day basis.

India must acknowledge the broader security needs in order to evolve comprehensive security machinery with clearly laid down concepts, carefully defined leadership roles and a workable co-ordination mechanism. In this broader view, the NSA has to play an active role, not only as an adviser to the prime minister, but also to the cabinet in matters relating to national security.

Laws and Legislation

Homeland Security and laws in The US Legislative Response After 9/11

(a) **Uniting and Strengthening America by Providing Appropriate Tools Required to Intercept and Obstruct Terrorism Act of 2001 (PATRIOT Act).** The Act drastically reduced the restrictions on law enforcement agencies' ability to search telephone, e-mail communications, medical, financial, and other records; eased restrictions on foreign intelligence gathering within the United States; expanded the Secretary of the Treasury's authority to regulate financial transactions, particularly those involving foreign individuals and entities; and broadened the discretion of law enforcement and immigration authorities in detaining and deporting immigrants suspected of terrorism-related acts. The act also expanded the definition of terrorism to include domestic terrorism, thus enlarging the number of activities to which the PATRIOT Act's expanded law enforcement powers can be applied. Among the important facets covered in the titles to the act is improved intelligence, enhancing domestic security, surveillance procedure, money laundering in support of terrorism, cyber terrorism and corruption in officialdom. Though the act initially invited controversy, with the adoption of most of the provisions by President Barack Obama, that controversy has greatly receded.

(b) **The Intelligence Reform and Terrorism Prevention Act of**

2004 (IRTPA). The act was enacted on December 17, 2004, and is an act of Congress that broadly affects US terrorism laws. In juxtaposition with the single-subject rule, the act is composed of several separate titles with varying subject issues. This act established both the position of DNI, the NCTC, and the Privacy and Civil Liberties Oversight Board (PCLOB). IRTPA addresses many different facets of information gathering and the intelligence community. Among the general provisions, the IRTPA modified many aspects of the federal intelligence and terrorism-prevention organizations as it:

- reorganized the Intelligence Community.

- established the position of DNI to serve as the President's chief intelligence adviser and the head of the Intelligence Community, and to ensure closer coordination and integration of the 16 agencies that make up the Intelligence Community (IC).

- established the NCTC to serve as a multiagency center analyzing and integrating all intelligence pertaining to terrorism, including threats to US interests at home and abroad.

- established the PCLOB as an independent federal agency—a 9/11 Commission recommendations.

- adopted the key principles of Executive Order 13356, strengthening the Sharing of Terrorism Information To Protect Americans, and directed the establishment of the Information Sharing Environment (ISE) and required the President to designate an ISE Program Manager.

- established the Information Sharing Council (ISC) to advise the President and the Program Manager about developing ISE policies, procedures, guidelines, and standards, and to ensure proper coordination among Federal departments and agencies participating in the ISE.

India's Legislative Response to 11/26.

(a) **The Unlawful Activities (Prevention) Amendment Act**

(UAPA). The 2008 legislative amendments intended to deal with terrorists, and adopted in haste following the November 2008 Mumbai terrorist attacks, were preceded by the Terrorist and Disruptive Activities (Prevention) Act 1987 (TADA), and the Prevention of Terrorism Act 2002 (POTA). Both TADA and POTA were criticized as draconian and anti-rights. TADA lapsed in 1995; the government decided not to extend the legislation following widespread protests. POTA was repealed in 2004, with the government recognizing that its provisions were being misused.

Both TADA and POTA were censured for being used as a control mechanism against minority groups in India. In 2004 the government introduced amendments to the UAPA, thus making it India's main anti-terror legislation. The December 2008 Unlawful Activities (Prevention) Amendment Bill further amends this Act and its amendments are criticized by experts as they merely borrow provisions from the previous anti-terror laws, rather than offering a new approach, in spite of the past failures of stringent anti-rights laws to curb terrorist attacks. The UAPA essentially further revised the old Unlawful Activities Prevention Act, 1967. Four new chapters essentially included 'terrorist activities' alongside 'unlawful activities', specifying different procedures to deal with each. With this substitution, specific provisions of POTA pertaining to definition, punishment and enhanced penalties for 'terrorist activities', and specific procedures, including the banning of 'terrorist organizations' and interception of telephone and electronic communications, were inducted into UAPA.[4] The major observations of discord and dissent range from the latest amendments of the definition of a terror act to arrest, pre-charge detention, bail application, proof of innocence, power over financial assets and freedom of movement. Terrorism legislation should have a life limited to a maximum, and require renewal by legislation. Experts have commented on the need for a periodic review and need for a sunset clause as in the case of the USA PATRIOT Act.

(b) **The National Investigation Agency Act.** National Investigation Agency (NIA) is a new federal agency approved by the Indian

---

[4] Ujjwal Kumar Singh, 'The State, Democracy and Anti-Terror Laws in India', Sage Publications, Delhi, 2007.

Government to combat terror in India. The agency will be
empowered to deal with terror related crimes across states without
special permission from the states. Post the 11/26 attacks, The NIA
Act, 2008 was formulated in the wake of the widespread criticism
of the government about alleged intelligence lapses leading to the
attack. The act states that notwithstanding anything in the Police
Act, the central government will constitute a special agency to be
called the NIA for investigation and prosecution of offences under
the acts specified in the 'Schedule'. The NIA also enables the central
government to constitute Special Courts.

NIA will have concurrent jurisdiction which empowers the Centre to
probe terror attacks in any part of the country, covering offences, including
challenge to the country's sovereignty and integrity, bomb blasts, hijacking
of aircraft and ships, and attacks on nuclear installations. Other than offenses
of terrorism, it will deal with counterfeit currency, human trafficking, narcotics
or drugs, organised crime (extortion mobs and gangs), and violations of
atomic energy act and weapons of mass destruction act. The agency is to
have a 'crime intelligence unit' like the CBI special crime unit, whose mandate
is to focus on terror related activities. The NIA will be linked to the MAC
(Multi Agency Centre) for information sharing among various intelligence
agencies. Experts again ask whether the Mumbai attacks, mostly critiqued
as a failure of intelligence, can be meaningfully addressed by the creation of
an investigative body (investigation being a post-event activity), managed
by upper level officers from the existing system that clearly could not prevent
such an attack.

It is significant that the statute deals with a national level 'investigation'
agency, as opposed to the refinement, reorganization and enhancement of
'intelligence' capacity. The Mumbai attacks, if anything, represent a failure
of intelligence gathering, i.e. warning systems to pre-empt such attacks.
Investigation usually connotes a police-based function, i.e. a post-fact
process. The point is that it is intelligence that provides leads which in turn
enable investigation by the police. The NIA statute instead focuses on
policing; it does not address intelligence lapses, the acute lack of expertise,
political infighting and absence of independence that define intelligence
agencies in India.[5]

---

[5] MenakaGuruswamy, 'Countering terror or terrorizing the law?',http://www.india-
seminar.com/2009/599.htm.

Intelligence

Intelligence and Homeland Security in America

Domestic Intelligence gathering in the US is still frowned upon and until recently was considered taboo. The events of the Dossier system and the Watergate scandal led to the dismantling of any structure connected with collection of intelligence within the country and stringent control was exercised on any specific requirements. The only investigative work was probably conducted by those involved in combating organized crime.

The IRTPA sought to remedy numerous problems uncovered by the 9/11 Commission, one of which was the gap between foreign and domestic intelligence. The IRTPA amended the National Security Act of 1947 to define the terms 'national intelligence' and 'intelligence related to national security' as all intelligence regardless of source from which derived and including information gathered within or outside the United States.

Since the 9/11 terrorist attacks, Congress has focused considerable attention on how intelligence is collected, analyzed, and disseminated in order to protect the homeland against terrorist threats. The distinction between "domestic intelligence" (primarily law enforcement information collected within the United States) and "foreign intelligence" (primarily military, political, and economic intelligence collected outside the country) today is blurred. Threats to the homeland posed by terrorist groups are national security threats, and intelligence collected outside the United States is often very relevant to the threat environment inside the United States and vice versa.

The 9/11 Commission stated that one of the challenges in preventing terrorist attacks is bridging the "foreign-domestic divide." The 9/11 Commission used this term for the divide that it found not only within the IC, but also between the agencies of the IC dedicated to the traditional foreign intelligence mission, and those agencies responsible for the homeland security intelligence and law enforcement missions. Charles Allen, the Chief Intelligence Officer of DHS, categorized security intelligence and law enforcement intelligence as "non-traditional" intelligence.[6]

DHS's Office of Intelligence and Analysis (I&A), a member of the Intelligence Community, ensures that any information related to protecting the homeland is collected, processed, analyzed, and disseminated to the full spectrum of domestic customers. It provides threat warning, estimative, and alternative analysis. In addition, it also provides intelligence support to infrastructure protection and vulnerability studies. I&A works closely with DHS component intelligence organizations to ensure non-traditional streams of domestic information are fused with traditional sources of information from other members of the IC to give a complete picture of potential threats to the nation. I&A has five analytic thrusts, aligned with the principal threats to the homeland: threats related to border security, threat of violent extremism, threats from particular groups entering the United States, threats to the Homeland's critical infrastructure and key resources, and weapons of mass destruction and health threats.

I&A contributes analytic staff to the NCTC. The office also contributes items to the President's Daily Brief and provides a homeland security perspective on terrorism and other threats to federal leaders. State, local, and tribal law enforcement—often described as the "first preventers" of terrorism— are another important set of customers. They require timely and actionable intelligence to respond to threats. They also need intelligence about the latest terrorist tactics and techniques so that they know what to look for and what to do when they encounter suspicious behavior or dangerous items. Finally, I&A is charged with supporting the operators of the nation's publicly and privately-owned critical infrastructure with threat information and other intelligence that supports their risk management decision making.

The I&A Under Secretary is a member of the DNI Executive Committee. The Under Secretary, in the capacity as Chief Intelligence Officer (CINT), implements a mandate to integrate DHS's intelligence components and functions.DHS's intelligence elements include: [7] US Citizenship and Immigration Services (USCIS), US Coast Guard (USCG),

---

[6] Mark A Randol, " Homeland Security Intelligence: Perceptions, Statutory Definitions and Approaches", Congressional Research Service report, January 14, 2009, p- 1.

[7] http://www.dhs.gov/xabout/structure

US Customs and Border Protection (CBP), US Immigration and Customs Enforcement (ICE), and Transportation Security Administration (TSA).

Intelligence and Homeland Security in India

Role of Intelligence. The concept of intelligence co-ordination and the role of intelligence in internal security management has many components.

- Intelligence collection within the country's frontiers.

- Trans-border intelligence collection.

- Intelligence collection in foreign countries.

- Use of technical means for the collection of intelligence specifically required for internal security management and also for external security.

Presently, there is no single ministry or department capable of coordinating all these roles leading to the observation that in India, the concept of an intelligence community has not evolved.

Similarly, the concept of leadership roles in security-related matters has not received attention. In America, under the Intelligence Community Act, all agencies are required to function as an organic whole.There is a consolidated intelligence budget for the community as a whole, prepared and presented for approval by the Congress by the DNI. The DNI makes individual allocations to different intelligence agencies. The leadership role in respect of counter-intelligence is with the FBI, in respect of counter-terrorism with the NCTC. The designated leaders coordinate the follow-up action.[8]

In his book *Intelligence: Past, Present and Future*, former R&AW official and Saxena Committee member B Raman pointed out the real problem plaguing the Indian intelligence set-up. Politicians, he pointed out, were cut off from the work of intelligence organizations, and most of them remained ill-educated about just what they were supposed to do, and were worse

---

[8] B.Raman, 'Revamping of The Internal Security Machinery' http:/ramanstrategicanalysis. blogspot.com.

informed about what they actually did. Raman argued that Parliament's Standing Committee on Home did receive briefings about the functioning of the IB, but few of its members had the requisite knowledge to ask tough questions and demand satisfactory answers. The situation suited everyone, including those in the intelligence world, who were happy with mediocrity. Until the political process took intelligence seriously, he suggested, Indian intelligence would never improve.[9]

Proposals for Intelligence Reform. The Observers Research Foundation (ORF), an Indian research body, has analysed the intelligence systems of several developed countries which have full legislative support like United States, the UK, Germany, Australia and others. The ORF report and the report of an earlier task force set up by the government under former R&AW chief Girish Chandra Saxena both suggest an urgent need for the government to enact legislation to improve the intelligence gathering system. The prime responsibility of intelligence gathering currently wrests with R&AW and IB.

The ORF report is in favour of allocating the IB responsibility for international security operations with a formal written charter. The Saxena report had earlier proposed promulgation of a written charter defining the mission of the R&AW. The Saxena panel believed that the concept of a viable intelligence community could only flourish when there was a proper coordination between different agencies based on formal written charters with minimal overlap in their functioning.[10] The ongoing friction between DHS and the US Department of Justice/FBI gives credibility to this belief. To empower intelligence agencies so that they are equipped with the tools and resources to address the challenges in the 21st century, the establishment of basic written charters governing their functioning is a must.

Bill on Intelligence Agencies Reforms. The Intelligence Services (Powers and Regulation) Bill has been introduced in the Budget Session of Parliament in March 2011 with an aim to regulate the functioning and use of power by the Indian intelligence agencies within and outside India and to

---

[9] Ibid

[10] *The Asian Age,* 21 Feb 2011, http://www.asianage.com

provide for the coordination, control and oversight of such agencies. The bill regulates the possible infringement of privacy of citizens while giving credence to security concerns. The bill provides for the following:--[11]

- A legislative and regulatory framework for the Intelligence Bureau, the Research and Analysis Wing and the National Technical Research Organisation.

- Designated Authority regarding authorization procedure and system of warrants for operations by these agencies.

- A National Intelligence Tribunal for the investigation of complaints against these agencies.

- A National Intelligence and Security Oversight Committee for an effective oversight mechanism of these agencies.

- An Intelligence Ombudsman for efficient functioning of the agencies and for connected matters.

The bill stipulates that the day-to-day operation of the R&AW shall be vested in an officer not below the rank of a Secretary to the Government of India. It also stipulates that the Intelligence Bureau shall function under the control of the Prime Minister. It mandates the IB to work for national security in the context of internal conflict and, in particular, provide protection against threats from espionage, terrorist acts organized by other countries within the territory of India with the help of Indian nationals or residents, and from actions intended to subvert the Constitution of India by violent means. The National Technical Research Organisation (NTRO) is to function under the control of the Prime Minister. The day-to-day operation of the NTRO shall be vested in a Chairman who shall be appointed by the Prime Minister.

The bill proposes a Committee, to be known as the National Intelligence and Security Oversight Committee, to examine the administration and compliance of policy laid down under the act. The Committee shall, unless it is necessary to perform the functions assigned to it under the Act, not go into the operational aspects and sources of intelligence of the functioning of

---

[11] Bill on Intelligence Agencies Reforms, 29 March 2011, http://www.observerindia.com.

the R&AW, the IB and the NTRO. The Committee shall comprise of among others the Prime Minister, Home Minister, leader of the opposition and prominent members of the Council of States.[12]

The Structure of DHS

The DHS combines and leverages the resources of federal agencies to create an integrated federal agency. The DHS components include TSA, CBP, and the Federal Emergency Management Agency (FEMA). The department also houses various advisory panels and committees. Secretary of Homeland Security Janet Napolitano has stressed the relevance of DHS working to expand efforts to build state and local level capacities to support four main priorities: the timely transmission of information and intelligence to states and local authorities; The recognition of terrorism related behaviour and picking up indicators by supporting the knowledge of the local authorities and the state agencies; the sharing of terrorism related suspicious activity among all levels of government; and the fostering a "whole of nation" approach to security through a vigilant public.

The threat is recognized to be not only from well known direct entities but also from homegrown violent extremism. The implication of homegrown terror has changed the focus from traditionally external spotting of terrorist activity to picking up signals and activity by the local and state law enforcers and frontline personnel. The four major tools to defend against terror plots are DHS Fusion Centers, DOJ Joint Terrorism Task Forces, and the Nationwide Suspicious Activity reporting (SAR) Initiative and the PATRIOT Act.

The FBI formed the National Security Branch with an Intelligence Directorate that focuses on counterterrorism. It has created Field Intelligence Groups (FIGs) focused on the analysis of intelligence. Each of the FBI's 56 field offices has a FIG collocated with it. However, the FBI is frequently criticized by local law enforcement for being too 'case oriented', which can conflict with its new role of being intelligence-driven.

---

[12] Ibid.

The FBI JTTFs are a mechanism created to jointly investigate terrorism cases and the task forces focus full time on preventing attacks and conducting counterterrorism investigations. They are staffed by FBI agents and employees from federal, state and local agencies. DHS also has personnel in some JTTFs. A total of 104 JTTFs across the US marshal the resources from numerous sources to conduct investigations. JTTFs operate at high levels of security classification. The work of JTTFs is highly investigatory in nature and has limited intelligence potential. Just as the Fusion Centers are analytical and information-sharing entities, the JTTFs are investigative teams that bring agencies together to investigate particular terrorism cases. The model is a workable model for investigation at both the federal and state levels. In some cases, the JTTFs and the Fusion Centers appear to be duplicative.

The DHS Fusion Centers are the analytical and information sharing entities that bring state and local agencies together to assess the implications of information received to generate a general threat picture. The 72 Fusion Centers facilitate the flow of intelligence reports and are the informers of terrorist threats, tactics, techniques and latest methods. These focal points for information sharing at all levels of government are located in many states and major urban areas. Fusion centers have a variance in their focus and capabilities in different states and cities, as they have morphed into "all threats, all hazard" centers. While some have gained significant capabilities as they have matured, others are nascent with few personnel having the requisite experience or training in intelligence.

To make the Fusion Centers a hub of useful and actionable information for identifying threats and alerting first responders, DHS has placed 68 experienced intelligence officers at the centers. DHS also provides support to the centers by grants and by deploying the Homeland Security Data Network (HSDN) to allow access to classified threat-related information. The training of personnel is thus crucial to the functioning of the centers and the network as a whole. DHS aims to achieve four baseline capabilities at the Fusion Centers:-

(a) The ability to receive classified and unclassified threat-related information from the federal government.

(b) The ability to assess the local implications of threat-related information through the use of risk assessments.

(c) The ability to further disseminate to localities the threat information so that law enforcement can recognize behaviors and indicators associated with terrorism.

(d) The ability to share appropriate locally-generated information with federal authorities to help identify emerging threats.

The SAR initiative, created by the Los Angeles Police Department, is one in which DHS and DOJ/FBI work closely to create a standard process for law enforcement to identify, vet and share reports of suspicious incidents or behaviors associated with the threat of terrorism. The program also trains frontline, analytic and executive personnel to recognize behaviors and indicators associated with terrorism and distinguish them from non-suspicious and legal behaviors. Over 13,000 federal, state and local law enforcement personnel across the US have received training so far. It is expected that virtually all frontline law enforcement personnel will receive this training by the end of 2011. The SAR Initiative also is installing information-sharing technologies within DHS that enable reports of suspicious activity that are vetted by specially trained analysts to be forwarded to JTTFs and Fusion Centers.

The Existing and Emerging Architecture in India

The present architecture consists of political, administrative, intelligence and enforcement elements. The Cabinet Committee on Security (CCS) is at the political level. The CCS consists of ex-officio ministers: the Prime Minister, HM Ministers of Defence, External Affairs and Finance. It is supported by the NSC, with representatives from the above ministries and the Deputy Chairman of the Planning Commission and National Security Adviser. The administrative element is the Ministry of Home Affairs, the Prime Minister's Office (PMO) and the Cabinet Secretariat.

The intelligence elements are spread over different ministries: the Intelligence Bureau (IB), the Research and Analysis Wing, the Joint Intelligence Committee (JIC), NTRO and Aviation Research Centre (ARC); the armed forces have their own intelligence agencies (one each under the

Army, Navy and Air Force); and an umbrella body called the Defence Intelligence Agency. Other agencies that specialise in financial intelligence are the Directorates in the Income Tax, Customs and Central Excise departments, the Financial Intelligence Unit, and the Enforcement Directorate. Because of the sheer number of entities, it is clear that no single authority spearheads a unified command that can issue directions to these agencies and bodies. This substantially reduces accountability in India.

The major connectivity in terms of intelligence between the central government and states is affected via the state offices of the IB and through the newly created Subsidiary Multi-Agency Centers (SMACs) via state police Special Branches. Under the Constitution, intelligence relationships relating to national security or investigations relating to the central government's jurisdiction or those relating to the newly created NIA, all exist according to the invitations and goodwill of the states. This artificial bifurcation of intelligence between state and central authorities constitutes a major impediment to the flow of intelligence between the grassroots and the central agencies. It is common knowledge that intelligence agencies everywhere are extremely poor at sharing intelligence, and India is no exception. They are restricted in doing so by different 'intelligence cultures', the existence of multiple agencies essentially doing the same thing (stove-piping), lack of trust and the natural desire to protect sensitive sources. Unfortunately, the police are particularly prone not to share intelligence for all the above reasons and because of a police culture that can often be skeptical of the intelligence function.

In the aftermath of the 11/26 attacks, the HM has already conducted a series of reforms and has outlined further major reforms. Reforms, either anticipated or accomplished, include synergizing the intelligence agencies to organize counter terror mechanisms, strengthening the border and coastal security, and modernizing the police force. Each of these aspects are detailed below.

(a) **Synergising Intelligence Agencies and Counter- Terrorism Mechanisms.** The Multi-Agency Centre (MAC), within the IB, has been re-furbished and strengthened. SMACs also have been established in the states. The MAC and SMACs are to be linked by a dedicated, secure network. In all, 30 locations (including the MAC, the SMACs and a number of police Special Branches) are to be linked by this network. A new, over-arching NCTC is to be created by end however is still awaiting government sanction and is still-born,. The NCTC will incorporate the MAC, NIA, NTRO, JIC, National Crime Records Bureau (NCRB) and NSG; have an operations division (presumably to include the NSG); and minimize the current bifurcation between agencies currently controlled by the NSA and the Ministry of Home Affairs.

To enable a more rapid response to major terror attacks than was achieved on 11/26, NSG hubs have been established in Hyderabad, Bengaluru, Chennai and Kolkata. Two additional regional response groups have been located in Hyderabad and Kolkata. Each hub is staffed by 250 people. The BSF has been significantly upgraded and re-equipped and 29 additional battalions are to be raised. The CRPF and other central paramilitary forces have also been significantly upgraded. The 21 existing, stand-alone databases will be networked through NATGRID for access to desired information for intelligence/enforcement agencies.

The exposure of serious gaps in the visa system by the Headley case has led to the proposal for Mission Mode Project (MMP). This will provide for online visa and foreigners' registration and tracking with the objective of creating a secure and integrated service delivery framework for facilitating legitimate travelers and strengthening security. It will be implemented over a period of four-and-a-half years. Funding for seven counter insurgency and anti-terrorism schools in five states has been allocated.

(b) **Strengthening of Coastal and Border Defences.** India has a coastline of 7517 kilometers of which more than 5400 kilometers is the length of the mainland coastline. The coastal security scheme is being implemented in two phases. With the full implementation of the first phase of the Coastal Security Scheme by March 2011, states and union territories will be better equipped in terms of coastal police stations (73), boats (204), vehicles (153), two-wheelers (312) and manpower and equipment including computers.

The second phase of the Coastal Security Scheme has also been finalized and approved. This phase will further supplement the states by providing more police stations (131), boats (180), large vessels, (10), jetties (60) and RIBs (35). The scheme will also provide support for equipment, such as computer systems, vehicles, and two-wheelers.

A uniform system for registration of all boats has been put in place. Action is also being taken for issuance of ID cards to all fishermen. A suitable command structure for maritime security has been firmed up with four joint operation centers being set up and placed under the Naval Commander-in-Chiefs. A SagarPrahariBal has been constituted and standard operating procedures (SOPs) for coastal security have been finalised in respect of all coastal states. There is increased emphasis on technology usage and the process of installation of transponders on vessels to ensure identification and tracking has been initiated. Radar chains are also being strengthened.

(c) **Modernizing the Police.**The Union government has assisted with funds for the recruitment of 400,000 additional state police. The government has promulgated guidelines for non-corrupt recruitment and developed an electronic system to ensure 'hands free' and non-corrupt recruitment. This system has already been implemented for central recruitment. The Union government is to assist with connectivity between police stations and the establishment of the Crime and Criminal Tracking Network System (CCTNS) which aims to facilitate collection, storage, retrieval, analysis, transfer and sharing of data and information at the police station and between the police station and the state headquarters and the central police organizations.

In addition to establishment of community policing, the plan is to organize and analyze information derived from the community and restructure the state police Special Branches as a specialized and self-sufficient cadre of the State police in terms of personnel, funds and equipment. In January 2009, the central government circulated a proposal to restructure the Special Branch in the State police forces. The implementation of the proposal will mark the beginning of an intensive effort to restructure the intelligence-gathering machinery at the district and state levels.

The Union Government will assist state police to establish 24x7 command and control posts and quick response teams (QRTs), properly equipped and trained. States are to establish and put into operation antiterrorism units (ATUs) to pre-empt and investigate terrorist attacks.

(d) **The Multi-Agency Centre (MAC).**The MAC, as an information aggregator anchored by the Intelligence Bureau, will be at the core of the NCTC. The government has nominated the MAC as the nodal agency for intelligence assessment. Every piece of relevant information or intelligence gathered by one of the participating agencies was to be brought to the table, analysed and the analysis shared with the participating agencies. The key benefit was that no one organisation was kept in the dark.

Another beneficial change has been the extension of the reach of MAC to the State capitals and the setting up of the subsidiary-MAC in each state capital in which all agencies operating at the state level, especially the Special Branch of the state police. Through the MAC-SMAC-State Special Branch network, the Intelligence Bureau has been able to pull more information and intelligence from the state capitals. It has also been able to push more information and intelligence into the state security system.

Initially, the functioning of MAC was supervised by the Home Minister himself. Earlier, meetings were attended by nominated nodal officers of intelligence agencies besides Central Paramilitary Forces (CPOs). However, it lost steam, with meetings a year later being attended by lower rank officers. Intelligence agencies share generic inputs with MAC, such inputs are vague, lack specificity and time frames and do not lead to any relevant assessment as gathered from observers. MAC, like all other intelligence agencies, is under-staffed to be functional round the clock and handles on an average 200 inputs every day.

Much like other intelligence entities, it suffers from a lack of institutional strengths to make timely assessments. It cannot "connect the dots" because it is not sufficiently imaginative. Bright officers and operatives have still not been posted, as each agency wants to retain its best manpower. There is a need of requisite incentives to send the best officers to intelligence-based appointments. Intelligence assessment and the coordination mechanism refurbished after 11/26 are not likely in a position to make timely and holistic assessments and assist in swift and coordinated response. It still lacks the teeth and unambiguous authority over Subsidiary Multi Agency Centers (SMACs) and state intelligence machinery.

(e) **National Investigations Agency (NIA).** The National Investigation Agency (NIA) under The National Investigation Agency Act was formulated in the wake of the widespread criticism of the current government about alleged intelligence lapses connected to the Mumbai attacks. Presently there exists only the provision for a Central Bureau of Investigation – an already existing overused and overworked body. The agency is to have a 'crime intelligence unit' like the CBI special crime unit, whose mandate is to focus on terror related activities. NIA will be linked to the MAC for information sharing among various intelligence agencies.

The NIA authorities draw their power essentially from the Unlawful Activities (Prevention) Act of 1967 and the new amendments that were passed soon after the Mumbai attacks. The amendments make three notable changes: in the definition of what is a terrorist act; in defining what is funding of terrorism and setting forth a punishment (minimum of five years to life imprisonment); and defining and punishing training of terrorists in camps, with a minimum sentence of five years extendable to life imprisonment.

The NIA is reportedly aspiring to have over 100 investigators, including 25 IPS officers. The agency is to have a 'crime intelligence unit' like the CBI special crime unit, whose mandate is to focus on terror related activities. NIA will be linked to the MAC for information sharing among various intelligence agencies.[13] The NIA

---

[13] Menaka Guruswamy, 'Countering terror or terrorizing the law?',http://www.india-seminar.com/2009/599.htm.

has the power to investigate throughout India any offences listed in its schedule. However, the NIA has not been given the necessary powers to preventoffences.

To properly prevent crime or terrorism it requires more than simply powers of investigation and enforcement. Provision has to be made for the sharing, collection, collation, analysis and dissemination of intelligence. In order for the NIA to be effective in preventing federal crime, it needs to be able to warehouse, process and coordinate the flow of critical information. The FBI was significantly restructured after 9/11 so that it could engage in, and collaborate with others on, counterintelligence activities. It was accepted that prevention is best served by the acquisition of information and then acting on that information. The Act is silent on information sharing, how information and intelligence is to be obtained, and on the NIA's relationship to other agencies that presently gather information. In fact, this oversight may severely compromise the NIA's ability to investigate Scheduled Offences, let alone prevent them.

Countering Terror

National Counter Terrorism Center (NCTC)

Investigations of the 9/11 attacks had demonstrated that information possessed by different agencies had not been shared and thus that different indications of the threat had not been connected and warning had not been provided. A central lesson from the 9/11 attacks was, inadequate interagency coordination in most part as a result of separate statutory settings and administrative hurdles.

In February 2002 the two congressional intelligence committees established a Joint Inquiry into the activities of the IC in the US connection with the terrorist attacks of 9/11 and concluded that, "for a variety of reasons, the IC failed to capitalize on both the individual and collective significance of available information that appears relevant to the events of September 11." The two intelligence committees recommended the establishment of an effective all-source terrorism information fusion center within the DHS to improve the focus and quality of counterterrorism analysis and facilitate the timely dissemination of relevant intelligence information, both within and beyond the boundaries of the Intelligence community.[14] Considerable concern revolved around the fact that DHS, as a new agency of the IC, would not be the best place for the integration of highly sensitive information from multiple government agencies.

In May 2003, the Terrorist Threat Integration Center (TTIC) was established without a statutory mandate to merge all threat information in a single location. DHS was a partner in TTIC and gradually came to concentrate on serving as a bridge between the national intelligence community and state, local, and tribal law enforcement agencies that had never been components of the national IC. Shortly after publication of the 9/11 Commission Report, an Executive Order based on constitutional and statutory authorities established the NCTC as a replacement of the TTIC.

The NCTC was to serve as the primary organization of the Federal Government for analyzing and integrating all intelligence possessed or acquired pertaining to terrorism or counterterrorism (except purely domestic terrorism) and serve as the central and shared knowledge bank on known and suspected terrorists. The NCTC according to the 9/11 Commission was expected to compile all-source information on terrorism and also undertake planning of counterterrorism activities, assigning operational responsibilities to lead agencies throughout the government. The NCTC would not just have the analytical responsibilities TTIC had possessed, it would also assign operational responsibilities to lead agencies for counterterrorism activities, but NCTC would not direct the execution of operations.

Strategic planning is to include the mission, objectives to be obtained, tasks to be performed, interagency coordination of operational activities, and the assignment of roles and responsibilities. However, NCTC may not direct the execution of such operations. According to publicly available information, NCTC provides intelligence in a number of ways including items for the President's Daily Brief and the National Terrorism Bulletin

---

[14] Richard A. Best Jr, 'The National Counterterrorism Center (NCTC)—Responsibilities and Potential Congressional Concerns', CRS Report for Congress, January 15, 2010, p- 1.

both of which are classified. NCTC claims to provide the Intelligence Community with 24/7 situational awareness, as well as terrorism threat reporting and tracking. NCTC maintains databases of information on international terrorist identities to support the government's watch listing system designed to identify potential terrorists.

NCTC products are available to some 75 government agencies and other working groups and facilitate information sharing with state, local, tribal, and private partners.[15] According to all available reports, NCTC has access to the databases of all intelligence agencies and it can draw upon analytical resources throughout the government to supplement its own files, but to what extent the disparate databases are technically compatible or whether they are, or can be, linked in ways that permit simultaneous searching is yet not clear

The Director of the NCTC would be appointed by the Director of Central Intelligence (DCI) with the approval of the President and with the advice and consent of the Senate. The position of the NCTC Director is unusual, if not unique, in government. The NCTC Director reports to the DNI for analyzing and integrating information pertaining to terrorism (except domestic terrorism) and for NCTC budget and programs. For planning and progress of joint counterterrorism operations (other than intelligence operations), however, he reports directly to the President. In practice, the NCTC Director works through the National Security Council and its staff in the White House.[16]

The Obama Administration has pointed to several specific failures by the counterterrorism community generally and NCTC in particular. The current role of the CIA's Counterterrorism Center and its effect on the NCTCs functioning leads to questions of beneficial or counterproductive competition between the two centers.[17] The NCTC's strategic analysis of the overall terrorist threat in recent times and the relationship between strategic analyses and operational planning also need to be under review. The NCTC's current

---

[15] Ibid, p-4.

[16] Ibid, p-7.

[17] Ibid, p-10.

role in dealing with different agency approaches to specific terrorist threats will need to be continuously assessed despite significant efforts to remove the "wall" between law enforcement and intelligence.

NCTC for India

Immediately after the Mumbai massacre in November 2008, India hurriedly established the NIA in order perhaps to be seen to be doing something. NCTC would perform functions relating to intelligence, investigation and operations. All intelligence agencies would therefore have to be represented in the NCTC. While the nature of the response to different kinds of terror would indeed be different and nuanced, NCTC's mandate is likely to be to respond to violence unleashed by any group – be it an insurgent group in the heartland of India or any group of religious fanatics anywhere in India acting on their own or in concert with terrorists outside India.

NATGRID and CCTNS would fall under the NCTC. The last function – operations – would be the most sensitive and difficult part to create and bring under the NCTC. The proposed 'operations' wing of the NCTC will give an edge – now absent – in the effort to counter terrorism. The establishment of the NCTC was expected to result in transferring some oversight responsibilities over existing agencies or bodies to the NCTC. Some agencies such as NIA, NTRO, JIC, NCRB and the NSG were proposed to be brought under NCTC and positioning of R&AW, ARC and CBI were proposed to be re-examined to place them under the oversight of NCTC to the extent that they deal with terrorism.

The Indian version of the NCTC is on the anvil, and it has to be formed in the shape of an overarching body that coordinates, evaluates and analyses all intelligence reports that relate to terrorism. The NCTC is expected to decide on a course of action and task the intelligence agency or any special forces that are made available for necessary action to abort the terrorist mission. The existing intelligence agencies are being proposed to become a part or even subordinate to the NCTC. The NCTC modeled on the US NCTC is expected to be an umbrella organization headed by an officer from the police or armed forces, which will have the triple responsibility of preventing, investigating and responding to terror attacks. Given the overarching responsibility of NCTC and its mandate, it is likely to be headed by a highly

qualified professional with vast experience in security related matters. The
NCTC is proposed to be part of a revamped, more compact and powerful
MHA. The cabinet note is prepared and awaits approval as per reports
which quote the HM.

Global Policing and Megacity Law Enforcement : Additional Lessons for India

Global criminals are almost always involved in crime within cities and have
established networks that can and are being increasingly used by potential
terrorists. The challenge for the modern day police forces is facing this
globalization of crime. Lieutenant John P. Sullivan of the Los Angeles
Sheriff's Department comments on how transnational criminal networks are
creating incentives to change traditional police operations and also describes
how law enforcement officers can better coordinate their activities as they
adapt to contain and eliminate global criminal threats and has called this
'Global Metropolitan Policing'.[18] The fusing of criminal and terrorist networks
has created a situation for policing where crimes have ramifications outside
of traditional police jurisdictions. India is more than familiar with the State
versus Centre reach of its law and order machinery and faces the same
problem of distinguishing between local, domestic and foreign threats.
Globalized terror and crime brings to fore the need to share expertise through
collaboratively and specifically engineered systems developed between police
forces of nations.

These links could foster information sharing and can be the basis for
more formal and legal arrangements. The New York Police Department
(NYPD) has reached out for information and perspective from sources around
the globe with a core team of skilled counter terrorists and created the
International Liaison Program (ILP), which assigns NYPD detectives to
work with local, national and international law enforcement agencies in
London, Paris, Madrid, Lyon, Tel Aviv, Amman, Abu Dhabi, Singapore,
Toronto, Montreal and Santo Domingo. These liaisons are the eyes and
ears of the NYPD gathering pertinent information on a daily basis and

---

[18] John P. Sullivan, ' Terrorism Early Warning and Co-Production of Counterterrorism
Intelligence', Canadian Association for Security and Intelligence StudiesCASIS -20th
Anniversary International ConferenceMontreal, Quebec, Canada,21 October 2005.

performing on-the-ground analysis that is relevant to keeping New York City safe.

There is considerable resistance to such initiatives from the FBI. Nevertheless, such liaisons are seen as the means to generate warnings and foster exchange of best practices between police forces in an effort to link and secure megacities. The linkages include intelligence organizations, nongovernmental organizations, and private and corporate security managements and aim to create a network of security-intelligence in an effort to defeat the networked crime and terror entities.

The Los Angeles Terrorism Early Warning Group (LATEW) is an organization that integrates criminal and other intelligence from all potential sources to help identify and provide early warning of threats to the city. TEW has developed a local network of Terrorism Liaison Officers (TLOs) at each law enforcement, fire service, and health agency in its area of operations. In addition, private sector counterparts, known as infrastructure Liaison Officers (ILOs) are also being established to ensure the flow of information between the TEW and key critical infrastructure and other entities. [19]

By the conduct of regular exercises within the city the activation of the TEW and the response to potential threats is tested, refined and new responses developed. The TEW model has been adopted in varying scales in numerous cities across the US and the efforts at expansion and coordination are supported by DHS. TEW is another emerging example of how networked intelligence and indicator detecting efforts are emerging in response to the networked nature of terrorism.

India has been the target of terror strikes and it is the megacities that have borne the brunt. The adoption of the concepts and tactics of the NYPD and LAPD can lead to the formulation of city specific TEW mechanisms in India. It is imperative that successful and viable working models be emulated with necessary local expertise. The teams could be headed by a city chief of counter terrorism and integrated with coordination with the SMACs and eventually the NCTC. The presence of a local police authority from the

---

[19] Ibid

megacities must be extended to ensure integration with local private industry and first responders such as hospitals and emergency services including the essential services sector. As crime and terror spill over national boundaries the extent of cooperation and liaison with partner nations and responsible neighbouring countries will effectively establish what many refer to today as global policing and counter-terror.

India – US Cooperation

India and the US are strategic partners today and both nations have taken progressive steps to strengthen their security cooperation. The turn round of the US view after 9/11 towards Indian assertions of Kashmir militants as terrorist was a important turning point. The US started describing terror events against Indian targets as part of global terrorism. The India-US Joint Working Group on Counterterrorism in 2000, revival of the India-US Defence Policy Group (DPG) in 2001, the Next Step in Strategic Partnership established in 2004 and the India-US Defence Framework Agreement in 2005 are indicators of forging of a mutual alliance. Through the Joint Working Group mechanism, the countries have exchanged information, training material, and methods related to interrupting terrorist financial networks, institutional and law enforcement steps to strengthen homeland security, border management and surveillance techniques, aviation security, and disaster management in the event of a terrorist incident involving weapons of mass destruction. [20]

As the cooperation widened, certain events led to a trust deficit between the two countries. Concerns of withholding of information of militants in Kashmir and terrorist links and reluctance to assist India in terror investigations in favor of sparing Pakistan embarrassment frustrated India. India's relations with Iran in 2005 during the Iran-US standoff were another impediment to the India-US nuclear agreement. The Indian view that the US withheld crucial intelligence in the terror attack on the Indian embassy in Kabul and US attempts to penetrate the Indian intelligence agencies raised intelligence sharing concerns in India.[21]

---

[20] U.S. Department of State, "India–U.S. 'Joint Working Group on Counter-Terrorism,'" January 24, 2002, at http://www.state.gov/r/pa/prs/ps/2002/7440.htm.

[21] Lisa Curtis, 'After Mumbai: Time to Strengthen U.S.–IndiaCounterterrorism Cooperation', Backgrounder published by The Heritage Foundation,No. 2217,December 9, 2008

US-India cooperation towards counter-terror reached new levels in the aftermath of the 11/26 Mumbai terror attack. US efforts to elicit cooperation from Pakistan in the investigations and information exchanges led to acknowledgement by Pakistan of the perpetrators being Pakistani. The FBI in turn had unprecedented access to evidence and intelligence from the Indian agencies. The cooperation extended to the Indian HM and his decision to model the Indian NCTC on the lines of the American agency points to the quiet and steady progress in the counter-terror attitudes of both partners.

The lack of vigorous action by the US against Pakistan for its involvement in the 11/26 strikes and the failure to pressure Pakistan to arrest and prosecute the ISI officers named by David Coleman Headley of the Lashkar's Chicago cell as involved in the 11/26 attacks has strengthened the belief of many observers in India that Pakistan believes that so long as it cooperates with the US against anti-US terrorists, the US will continue to turn a blind eye to its use of the Lashkar brand of terrorists against India. This misunderstanding between the intelligence professionals of the two countries has arisen from the alleged reluctance of the FBI to give independent access to Headley to Indian investigators for interrogation and from a perception that that the FBI has not been as forthcoming as it ought to have been and has not shared with the Indian investigators all the information that needed to be shared. To both reconstruct the events of 11/26 and to prevent future attacks it is imperative to accept that this case may be one of many planned and calls for the intelligence communities to cooperate without looking back to the causes of previous rancor.

To put the relations in perspective over the last decade it is evident that the events of 9/11 turned out to be one turning point and the attack of 26/11 is turning to be the second cornerstone in the relationship. In the short and long-term, bilateral cooperation will remain a high priority issue for both nations and measures need to be taken to remove circumspection due to perceived differences. Cooperation in combating homegrown terror and violence by Maoists in India are future thrust areas. Measures such as establishing official mechanisms for counter-terror meetings, training, data management and other governmental level initiatives can also be accompanied by strengthening private high value industry protection mechanisms and increasing private interface with existing official channels. [22] Joint evaluations and encouragement in both countries to independent research groups could lead to better management and nuanced approaches in the respective nations while learning from each other's experiences.

Conclusion

The transformation the Indian internal security architecture is undergoing is considered by many to be a revolution and in many ways mirrors the changes undertaken in the US since 2001. This replication stems from the early assistance the FBI provided in the immediate aftermath of 11/26 in Mumbai and the many visits by Indian leaders and top bureaucrats to the US to understand the mechanisms and structure adopted. There are differences though in the manner in which the reforms are being applied and emerging in India.

The proposed Indian NCTC, will be structurally somewhat different from the US model. It is proposed the HM and not the NSA will be the approximate counterpart of the American DNI. This is a significant difference, since under the Indian model there will be no single intelligence head having authority over all government intelligence agencies. The domestic agencies involved with intelligence, such as the IB and NIA, will be organizationally separated from the foreign intelligence agencies and military agencies and all such intelligence is proposed to be fused in the MAC, which will be located within the NCTC.

The NCTC was conceptualised to house the MAC, the NIA, the IB and government response agencies, such as the NSG. It is here the connection between intelligence and counter-terrorism operations will be established. The effectiveness of the operations of the MAC potentially provides an area of weakness in the model as its effectiveness dictates success. It also means that the gap between domestic and external intelligence may not be

---

[22] Polly Nayak, 'Prospects for US-India Counter-terrorism cooperation: An Historical Perspective', Counter Terrorism in South Asia, ORF- Heritage Dialogue, KW Publishers Pvt Ltd, New Delhi, p38-41.

adequately bridged in the Indian case. The military related agencies work under the Ministry of Defence and are additional cause for such gaps.

Other components, such as state police first response, post event investigations, management of the terror event and arrangements for those arrested, rest predominantly within the jurisdiction of individual states. Many other important concerns about policing, governance and accountability need to be addressed because the state and grassroots levels are key elements in counterterrorism and counter-insurgency. One important measure relevant to police and law enforcement is the collection and maintenance of sound law enforcement and crime statistics. Statistics are fundamental to accountability and strong, inter-linked statistics between courts and the police are capable of furnishing key information about both court and police performance. The establishment of the CCTNS should be a priority towards this end.

The IB and the NCTC through the MAC, will have links into the states via its state offices and the SMACS, which will in turn have links with the state police Special Branches. These links, however, are likely to be indirect and incomplete. The strength of the links and their usefulness can only be optimized if the proposed modernization of the police force progresses in the central police and police forces of all states.

The main police body within the NCTC will be the NIA. The NIA is, however, a strictly limited agency that will not have the capacity according to its current legislation to provide the link between the intelligence agencies and state police. However, main issue with the NIA Act is that it does not support the intelligence collection process – which is in turn essential for prevention. It is essentially concerned with an offence reported as a FIR. But intelligence is not about offences or evidence. It is information surrounding potential offences that will need to be collected by local-level police and passed upward through the intelligence process. The grassroots police functionaries will have to gather this in effective community policing.

Grassroots intelligence in the present setting will sporadically be passed between Special Branches, the SMACs and the MAC, and if it is, it will continue to be a hit- and- miss process, and crucially, the intelligence feed from the grassroots will only be as good as the police providing it. The present reform process indicates that the process of state-level policing will be a long time progressing from the present paramilitary thrust that the police force has. The government will need to ensure that police reforms remains a major priority in its security reform process and that it does not get pushed aside by other quick fix reforms and remains in focus over the long-term. Cooperation with countries that have fine-tuned policing and global policing techniques must be integral to the police modernization and reforms presently underway.

The HM has proposed broad areas of change: making the MHA exclusively responsible for Internal Security and its management; creation of the NCTC; and, effective control of the coast and borders by tightening immigration. The principle behind the decentralized nature of the US structure needs to be kept alive to avoid the MHA from becoming too central to IS and intelligence. The functions of intelligence, counter terror and coordination of physical security must be separate and yet each agency must be held accountable in an interlinked architecture by law. It is proposed that the National security architecture for dealing with both internal and external threats to national security including terrorism must be debated in parliament to arrive at a political and administrative consensus of change and eliminate turf guarding. This debate will ensure that strengthening of counter terrorism capabilities does not adversely affect the focus of each individual agency towards other specific national security priorities that they specialize in.

5

Countering Insurgency in South Asia: Different Approaches

Brigadier Amrit Pal Singh

Introduction

This paper focuses on three "live" cases in Afghanistan, Pakistan and India (which has had more than one ongoing insurgency). The name given to the operations to counter the variants of insurgency differs from Low Intensity Conflict (LIC) in Pakistan and India,who tend to follow the British nomenclature, to Counter-Insurgency (COIN) a term of American origin. Regardless of the name or term applied, the importance of the strategic and political context and the operational strategy of these "small wars"are reflected upon, as is the nature of the insurgents and the internal and external support they receive.

The US is currently focused on assisting Afghanistan in establishing a form of governance that is stable, thereby denying terror groups a base to operate from. In India the focus of the government is to provide governance, which fosters economic growth and livelihood to the people of Jammu and Kashmir, along with pacifying the lingering insurgencies of the Northeastern region or in the *Naxalite* heartland along a belt in Eastern India. Pakistan is involved in an internal struggle to tame multifaceted terror unleashed by years of providing support to proxy insurgents in neighbouring Afghanistan and India. The three different approaches to COIN reflect wide variation, but also the potential of commonalities and lessons for the future.

This paper analyses three different approaches to COIN in South Asia, contrasting the ISAF-led efforts to tackle the Taliban in Afghanistan, with the Pakistani and Indian experiences to deal with local insurgencies, including in the Federally Administered Tribal Areas (FATA) and in Jammu and Kashmir. These three approaches are evaluated across eight different dimensions, including the doctrine, experience and scope of COIN activities; operational preferences and traditions; paramilitary organisational innovations; use of supportive force such as air power, artillery and technology; the political dimensions and civil-military relations; and strategies of reconstruction and reconciliation.

The findings suggest that while non-institutionalized and diffuse, the historical Indian experience holds valuable lessons for US COIN objectives in Afghanistan, and perhaps also in Pakistan.

Thought: Background, Doctrine and Strategy

The Indian Experience

It is impossible to look at Indian COIN without taking the pre-Independence experience of the British *Raj* into account. The British Indian Army conducted military operations in the Naga Hills as early as 1875 to confront tribal revolts. The British also conducted operations in frontier areas of British India, most of which are now part of Pakistan. The operations there were mainly directed to contain the influence of the various Pashtun tribes and to create a buffer zone between India and Afghanistan. Conventional expeditionary forces usually moved into the rebellious area to suppress the tribes through swift actions and then depart immediately. Unlike post-Independence operations by Indian regiments, which reflected the objectives of minimum use of force, and of respect for local customs and traditions, the British imperial authorities tended to be punitive and left behind a legacy of colonial abuse.[1]

---

[1] Maj-Gen. (retd) Dipankar Banerjee, 'The Indian Army's counter insurgency doctrine' in *India and Counter Insurgency*, SumitGanguly and David P Fidler (eds.); Routledge, 2009; p. 190.

In the Initial years after independence, following partition and the emergence of the low-intensity conflict (LIC) in Kashmir, India responded to insurgencies with the rather primitive view that they were caused by the formation of new political states or by "misguided youth". However, over time, efforts to control the insurgency led to a gradual increase in deployment of the army by the central government, not only in Kashmir, but also in many of the Northeastern states, where the armed and paramilitary forces were often perceived as occupiers. The army functioned under strict orders for preservation of the human rights and respectful treatment of innocents. An early *diktat* on the minimum use of force has probably been inspired by Jawaharlal Nehru'sopposition to use of force against his own countrymen.

Beyond its strict military functions, the army often also operated under the Armed Forces Special Powers Act (AFSPA), thus replacing inexistent or insufficient local police and law and order machineries. Since then, the Indian army has been increasingly deployed in the early stages of militancy to control the spread of violence and terror. India had to deal with insurgencies in the Northeastern states (mainly in Nagaland, Mizoram, Tripura and Manipur) and in Punjab, mainly in the 1970s and 80s, where it achieved success. India has faced rebellions and secessionist movements since its inception as a nation and has as a matter of record still managed to keep the level of violence limited and low along with restoring a degree of normalcy in the affected regions.

The COIN experience in India has evolved around common threads of principles and objectives: domination of the affected areas by strong military presence, isolation of the militants, use of minimum force, efforts to restore normalcy to the areas and finally assist and hand over administration to the state government. A conventional war bias often noted in the Indian Army's COIN operations is that of reluctance to innovate in doctrine. The numerous insurgencies have never won against the state – a notable feather in India's cap considering that common wisdom espouses that insurgencies can never be won. Starting from the early insurgencies in Nagaland and Mizoram the Indian strategy has been focused on the use of minimum force. This guiding principle has governed the employment philosophy of the army and is the cornerstone of the army doctrine on sub conventional operations.

However, despite being involved in COIN for over 60 years, there has been no single synthesis of the experiences of the Indian Army. A rare codification of the accumulated experience has resulted in *The Doctrine on Sub Conventional Operations* promulgated in 2006. The categorization of operations it offers encompasses the range of conflicts from armed conflicts that are above the level of peaceful coexistence to those below the threshold of war.

The civilian side in India has not shown signs of systematic thought on COIN and the document is seen by certain experts as an attempt to nudge them into conceptualization by providing a rational, harmonized and centralized doctrinal guidance on COIN.[2] The doctrine states the need for management of conflicts by a multi-pronged thrust by all elements of national power. The security forces are used in the initial stages to provide a secure environment for the government agencies whose activities were disrupted by violent acts of the militants. The doctrine enunciates the clear limits to use of force and the centrality of efficient civil–military cooperation. It also prioritizes the resource allocation, acquisition and training initiatives in the form of specific guidelines.

The ISAF experience in Afghanistan

The "trilemma" of Lorenzo Zambernardi underlined the implicit tradeoffs involved in any counterinsurgency operation.[3] The three goals of force protection, differentiation between enemy combatants and non-combatants, and elimination of insurgents, are not simultaneously achievable and it is precisely this "trilemma" that the ISAF leadership now faces in Afghanistan. The choice has been to differentiate between combatants and non-combatants in a foreign land, amongst tribals and wide ethnic complexity, which poses as a great risk to the safety of the ISAF troops involved in operations to eliminate insurgents. The extension of the COIN strategy of "clear-hold-build-transfer" from the Iraq experience to Afghanistan is a conscious choice

---

[2] David P. Fidler, 'The Indian Doctrine for Sub-conventional Operations', in *India and Counter Insurgency*, SumitGanguly and David P. Fidler (eds.); Routledge, 2009; p. 211.

[3] Zambernardi, Lorenzo, "Counterinsurgency's Impossible Trilemma", *The Washington Quarterly*, 33:3, July 2010, pp. 21-34

thatacknowledges this tradeoff. The protection of the population and the elimination of insurgents have increased the exposure of the combat forces to risk and sacrifice thereby raising casualties and leading to increased scrutinyby the administration and a gradual drop in public support to the war effort.

The destruction in the early phases of Operation Enduring Freedom (OEF) has given way to the hold and build phase. The change in approach to the war in Afghanistan from the characteristic American intent of uncompromising destruction of enemy forces to one of a more finely tuned harnessing of military effect, also to serve political means, has evolved through the operational and strategic lessons of Iraq which were critical in finalizing the COIN doctrine as employed in Afghanistan. The present strategy aims to assist the Afghan government in denying terrorists the use of the country as a base.

The strategy of clear and hold is proving to be a difficult one to execute on the ground, especially given the ability of terrorists to infiltrate, intimidate fence sitters and regroup constantly. The bread and butter operations have therefore been the cordon and search operations at battalion and unit level,intensified by aggressive employment of Special Forces operations for intelligence-guided precision actions. With the battle in Afghanistan extending to the South of the country, ISAF forces are also increasingly conducting road opening and convoy protection operations.

The surge of 2010 has had mixed support in the political landscape of the United States. What the increased military presence offers is the ability to organize a concerted effort towards moving the various Afghan factions in the conflict towards the negotiating table. According to Bernard Finel, the best option for the US is to use the approximately100,000 troops presently deployed in Afghanistan to bludgeon, cajole and coerce the insurgent forces and use the deployment to best effect from a position where maximum strength may not have yet been achieved but as strength and control of areas increases relatively.[4] He calls this strategy as a "Talk and Fight" strategythat

---

[4] Bernard I Finel, ' Planning a Military Campaign to Support Negotiations in Afghanistan', smallwarsjournal.com, October 2010

increases pressure on insurgents by tailored military operations to support negotiations. This kind of use of military force calls for a careful calibration of application of force to induce insurgents to negotiate, for example by making one faction or another face the brunt of operations to cause fissure in the insurgent coalition and provide the Afghan government the negotiation capability.

The primacy of military force as the central pillar of COIN allows for additional diplomatic leverage to be applied in addition to other *softer* modes of employment of power, including people-centric operations. This multi-level approach is emerging as the consensual COIN doctrine in South Asia, and is actually confirmed by the Indian and Pakistan COIN experience in the subcontinent.

Pakistan: where it all started

The US-led invasion of Afghanistan became the reason for the move of Taliban and Al-Qaida leaders into the Federally Administered Tribal Areas (FATA) of Pakistan. This region was created by the British as a buffer zone between British India and the then kingdom of Afghanistan, and extended from Peshawar in the North to Baluchistan in the South. Since then, the area has been inhabited by local tribes which survived in the rugged terrain that essentially persisted as a no-man's-land. The Soviet invasion of Afghanistan led to large refugee camps being established across the porous borders and it was from these camps that the Mujahedeenwere recruited for the US-backed effort against Soviet forces.The support for the religious leaders in an Islamic war against the Soviet invaders was the basis for the rise of the religious schools – madrassas– that served as breeding grounds for the holy warriors of Islam.The tribes provided all support to the Mujahedeen fighters – first against the Soviets and then against their ethnic kin – to achieve control over Kabul. Arab fighters joined the anti-Soviet effort and the rise of the Taliban after the Soviet withdrawal enabled the emergence of the pan-Islamic movement that was later explored by Al-Qaida.

The post-9/11 invasion by the US, with Pakistan as the main partner in what was then referred to as the Global War on Terror, led Pakistan's army to deploy its troops to secure the border with Afghanistan. The forces deployed were strike formations from the Eastern border with India and not trained for, nor having any operational experience inthis new context. Terrain knowledge or intelligence about local population was scarce. The short time available to deploy precluded any possibility to raise new or reorient existing Pakhtun regiments with local knowledge and ability to speak the language. The rugged terrain, a long border, shortage of troops to man innumerous border posts, coupled with little knowledge of the local customs and language, led to an ineffective control of the areas.[5] The isolated posts in tribal-dominated areas often resorted to deals to guarantee their sustainability and thus largely compromised the militaryobjectives to deny insurgents the possibility to use FATA as their safe haven.

The traditional focus of the Pakistan army has been India, which is perceived as the "real" threat and led to the glorification of the army as the protectors against India. This bias is the likely cause of the importance assigned to armour and infantry in conventional roles. Frontier warfare – a term coined by British – remains a neglected aspect in the Pakistani army curriculum. The army was ill equipped for COIN and also lacked mobility on the few narrow frontier roads, all the while insurgents operated four wheel drive trucks and converged on isolated posts to subdue them. The early operations by the army were not sufficiently aggressive and attempted to dominate areas by its sheer passive presence. This space-domination tactic, as well as sidelining of tribal elders caused alienation of the population, which in turn led to further recruitment possibilities for the Taliban and Al-Qaida. The inadequately trained and equipped army was thus forced to get involved in deals with the local commanders of the tribal militia in Waziristan and in the NWFP region.

Pakistan has tackled COIN more by coercion and only sometimes with limited degrees of political reconciliation after military operations.The initial operations by the Pakistan army were a mix of area domination and occupation of areas. Later attacks like the one in Bajaur were fierce,with attacks by artillery and even air strikes,reducing large areas to rubble. The insurgents' use of suicide bombings, IEDs and small group attacks soon

---

[5] Shuja Nawaz, 'Learning by Doing-The Pakistan Army's Experience with Counterinsurgency', Atlantic Council, February 2011, p-7.

[6] Haider Ali Hussein Mullick, 'Lions and Jackals-Pakistan's Emerging Counterinsurgency Strategy',*Foreign Affairs*,July 15, 2009.

inflicted heavy losses and increased the violence. The Pakistan Army initially
followed a policy of clearing an area of insurgents and handing the areas to
local governments and police.[6] This reluctance to hold cleared areas,
outsource governance and not focusing on development initiatives such as
roads, schools, security and jobs, eventually led to the capitulation of the
weak local authorities. The fierce pressure generated by the insurgents
caused the local authorities to enter into deals with the insurgents and they
allowed them to establish bases, eliminate collaborators and carry out
recruitment.

A particular variant of the "separate-fish-from-the-water" approach
was repeatedly used by the Pakistani army in Bajaur, in 2008. Large areas
were cleared of civilians by moving them out of towns and villages and then
attacking the area with air and artillery assaults in something akin to the
scorched earth technique- only that this was applied on home ground. The
resultant displacement of population and reconstruction efforts posed another
humanitarian crisis in the wake of army operations. The spin off though
was a wave of victories and surrender of key Taliban warlords leading to
the establishment of writ of the government. In 2009 the situation in Swat
flared up when the Taliban broke the peace agreement, but this time the
local and political consensus was with the army, which conducted operations
and implemented the lessons learned from Bajaur. A more people-centric
approach and recognition of the Taliban as the existential threat paid dividends
operationally and also recovered the image of the army as a respected national
agency.

The COIN-FOIN paradox. Haider Mullick suggests that Fomenting
Insurgency (FOIN)along with Countering Insurgency (COIN) are both part
of Pakistan's national security calculus.[7] FOIN in the 1980s was directed
against the Soviet occupation and was a creation of US and Pakistani
intelligence and security assets to bolster the Afghan mujahedeen.Over a
period of time in the late 1990s, as Pakistan's proxy, the Taliban had control
over Afghanistan and the FOIN operations extended to Kashmir and Punjab

---

[7] Haider Ali Hussein Mullick, 'Pakistan's Security Paradox: Countering and Fomenting
Insurgencies', JSOU Report 09-9, December 2009, U.S. Joint Special Operations
University,

in India. This support has engulfed the region in constant conflict and given rise to radical non-state actors which Pakistan admits have been responsible for the 2008 Mumbai and 2001 Parliament attacks in India.

A dual policy wherein it treats the Afghan Taliban as leverage and Pakistan Taliban as enemies of the state has thus given rise to the "good" and "bad" Taliban differentiation within the Pakistani establishment. This effectively implies that the Afghan Taliban, who are seen as patrons of Al Qaida, are patronized and provided asylum in Pakistan and that only the Pakistani Taliban, comprising of terrorists and Punjabi militants, are targeted by the army. The paradox of both FOIN and COIN within the Pakistan policy creates a disconnect between the US and Pakistani operational objectives in the region. As US forces struggle with a weak ANA to reduce the influence of the Taliban in Afghanistan, the Pakistan army has had reasonable success- at least in military operations - in Swat and Waziristan against the Pakistan Taliban.

Scope: In and out of Country

As highlighted with US forces that are deployed in Afghanistan, the conduct of operations in a foreign land imposes severe logistic and manpower constraints. The armies of Pakistan and India are operating in their own country and face these problems to a much lesser degree. The greater distance not only imposes greater logistic costs but also limits the number of effective troops available for the conduct of actual day-to-day COIN. The US experience in such overseas deployments post-World War II, for example in Korea and Vietnam, imposed such severe strain on the deployment, leading to results or outcomes that were far from decisive. The ongoing engagements in Iraq and Afghanistan, where 150,000 troops of the 1.5 million active duty personnel are deployed, is a challenge in maintaining an effective of combat support versus combat ratio.[8] The hindrances of overseas operations are logistic, strategic and tactical in nature. The shortage of numbers due to logistic impediments is compounded by the core weakness of tactical intelligence against an enemy who exploits the advantage of terrain and

---

[8] George Friedman , 'Never Fight a Land War in Asia', URL: http://www.stratfor.com/weekly/20110228-never-fight-land-war-asia.

local knowledge. American strategy of defining a mission and clarity on termination of intervention faces severe challenges when persecuting operations overseas.

The Indian COIN experience ranges from the Northeastern states, Punjab and Kashmir to overseas theaters such as in Sri Lanka, after 1987. The long presence of the army in the affected areas has led to a degree of permanent infrastructure and logistic efficiency as operations have unfolded. The deployment of the army is generally in all states with a bias towards the Western and Eastern borders, given the tenuous relations with the neighbouring countries in the region. The army deployments thus have evolved to a configuration of combining COIN with standard rotation of units in conventional duties from one sector to another. Since most headquarters and logistic installations are permanent or semi- permanent the teeth-to-tail ratio is kept positive.

Pakistan, on the other hand, has had little or no experience with COIN until after 2001. The East Pakistan (now Bangladesh) experience and the sporadic insurgency in Baluchistan of 1973 did not do much in terms of providing vital experience or operational knowledge regarding generation of an advantage in logistic, training or tactical operations. The Soviet experience in which jihad was exported from Pakistan, and the later diversion of jihad to Kashmir, did not contribute to operational learning from COIN due to control of those operations mostly by the ISI with US support. Prior to 9/11 the only troops in the Federally Administered Tribal Area (FATA) region were under a paramilitary force called the Frontier Corps (FC), officered by the Pakistan Army.

The movement and deployment of troops to SWAT, which culminated in operations in 2008, was a new and hastily imposed deployment to areas where the army had no detailed presence till then. The army faced a wave of resentment and was branded as alien when it moved in after 9/11 and was perceived by the locals to be doing the bidding of the US. The logistics of deployment all along the frontier abutting Afghanistan with limited mobility on ground due to the terrain and limited air resources resulted in a rather porous and ineffective sealing of the border.

The efficacy of control especially political control over outcomes in

COIN in a foreign country is a major consideration to measure effectiveness. The advantage Indian COIN efforts enjoy with a consistent politicalpolicy towards the resolution of conflict contrasts starkly with the efforts of the US which has to contend with the nascent government in Kabul which contributes with sporadic control of the National effort. Pakistan on the other hand is handicapped by the ineffective nature of the control that the government has in the FATA and other border areas which leads to tribal and other Taliban groups challenging the writ of the state.

Action: Operations and Deployment

Evolution of Indian COIN operations

Insurgency in India has its origins right after the 1947 partition, when the Naga rebellion in the Northeastern state of Nagaland led to the employment of the army. The predominantly British experiences have had an influence on the army's professional view of COIN and have tended to influence early operations, such as in the Naga case in the 1950s. However, the British Malaya model of village resettlement proved to be less than successful when applied by the Indian army. Two factors- external support to the insurgents and the distinctive difference between Malaya of the British and Nagaland, Mizoram of India- proved to the Indian army that the British model was not applicable to the Northeast.The nascent civilian administrative authorities also gained experience and of the role in of COIN and a strategy of political accommodation, instead of outright military victory, emerged from this rebellion and the subsequent Mizo rebellion of 1966. Reflecting this experience, current Indian COIN thinking firmly reflects the conviction that insurgencies are primarily political problems that need a political solution and military operations can only *assist* in setting the stage for the final political resolution. Operations by the army also reflect the assimilation of the attitude of minimum use of force and conduct of operations with immense limitations regarding employment of heavy equipment such as artillery and airsupport.

An important element of COIN by the Indian Army has been the reliance on dominance of the areas by concentration of troops. The army has been in the lead role in controlling operations of the central police forces and paramilitary forces such as the Assam Rifles and Border Security Force battalions assigned by the central government to the insurgency affected areas. The lack of heavy firepower has always been made up by asserting control by blanketing the area of operations. The central idea of the use of large-scale deployments has smothered notions of success nurtured by the insurgents and psychologically dented them by the sheer *magnitude* of the force.Operations are generally conducted in large numbers of manpower, as opposed to the general notion of small unit operations which has now been gradually adopted. Cordon and search operations involving more than one battalion of infantry have been a common practice.

This approach to COIN probably displays a conventional bias of the Indian army that is still dominant in the psyche of the army's thinkers, mainly due to the rotational nature of the army's deployments of its battalions from conventional role to a COIN role. The weapons and equipment primarily are designed for conventional operations and units have over a period of time acquired specialist equipment when employed in COIN. Operational learning over repeated deployments has got institutionalized into the doctrine for sub-conventional operations.

Operations by the security forces focus on sealing of borders to stop trans-border movement of militants and their supplies, establishment of a comprehensive counter terror grid in the hinterland, denial of population centres to militants securing military lines of communications with protection of vulnerable areas. The mere deployment of the security forces is a signal towards zero tolerance of violence and concerted tactical operations towards isolating and neutralizing the militants. At times the security forces have struck openly and hard against the militants to convey the determination of the government. However, such actions are perpetuated strictly in consonance with the laws of the land with full opportunity for the militants to surrender. Operations aim to induce support for civil governance within the ranks of the vast majority of fence sitters within the local population.

The use of intimidation and coercion by the militants is a recurring phenomenon and is taken advantage of by rogue and criminal elements – sometimes hand in glove with corrupt administration, politicians and police officials. The criminal-political- insurgent nexus is a live issue and calls for an understanding of the nuanced realities in Kashmir where COIN for some is now an industry, a means to coerce the system with the threat of resurgence of violence.

In the field, as any Indian Army company commander will testify, the drill of getting ready for a day or night in the Kashmir Valley starts with a weapon check and the quick final briefing. In between looking after the safety of his small team, a patrol leader also checks communications and works out contingencies and reinforcement plans for every foray into the Area of Responsibility (AOR). The ultimate desire of a junior leader is for a clean contact and ability to ensure fire discipline during contact. He also hopes for relative peace on the radio as he conducts the firefight -- a situation not always guaranteed when headquarters at various levels get involved in micromanaging operations. The aim of neutralizing the militants by elimination or capture alone is not a measure of overall success of operations as the dangers of becoming a "strategic corporal" are clear and present in everyday actions. The officers today understand that factors such as generation of actionable intelligence, degree of groundswell of public support for civic projects and minimization of seditious media reports in the AOR all go towards crediting the establishment of governance by the state government's institutions.

Operation Enduring Freedom (OEF)

The ISAF operations in Afghanistan have undergone four stages of transition from the early phase of 2001 which ended in the December 2001 complete victory by the small Special Forces- CIA contingent and Army teams that dominated operations for the four months after September 12, 2001. The second stage of operations was from January 2002 with a modest footprint of 4000 troops that gradually grew to a 20000 strong force. Operations were sporadic and sometimes intense as the escalation that took place in 2006 (when as the bombs dropped steeply increased from a mere 82 in 2004 to 3500 in 2006) displayed. The US tried to disengage from leadership in Afghanistan in December 2006 and operational command was assumed by NATO. This new stage saw no increase in troop levels but was characterized by a lack of effective command of operations with far too many hands on the steering wheel as remarked by Lieutenant General David W. Barno who once commanded the Combined Forces Command in Afghanistan. It is likely that the commitments in Iraq had put a severe constraint on the facilities and troops available in this war. From early 2008 the US assumed command of COIN with a gradual increase of force levels which led upto the surge of the summer of 2010 when the troop levels went to approximately 10000. Another consequence of the constant shift in command was gathering a unity of effort in operations and in the non- military sphere. The frequent changes of commanders as the military structure evolved unevenly and the different chains of command of the military commanders and civilian ambassadors - 10 military commanders and six ambassadors have changed in the 10 years of the operations –had adverse second and third level effects caused on operational effectiveness.[9]

Operations by the coalition forces against the Taliban can also be broadly classified into two distinct phases based on the type of operations being executed. Phase one of operations commenced with an air campaign on October 7, 2001with massive air strikes against ground forces. The Taliban were organized as military units and deployed conventionally against the Northern alliance with tank and some artillery support. The air campaign supported later by special operations teams inserted on the ground caused serious attrition to the Taliban which was disposed in traditional fighting positions. The ground war saw the conventional superiority of the coalition forces overrun Kunduz, Mazar-i-Sharif and Kabul in quick coordinated operations with the support of some Afghan tribes.

This conventional bias of an otherwise asymmetric organization led to its rout. The subsequent operations in the Tora Bora caves were a coordinated and concerted effort in which large casualties were suffered by the Taliban, however, a clear victory did not emerge and the Taliban switched to dispersed fighting and used the inhospitable terrain and porous border with Pakistan to melt away to fight another day. The Coalition also included the Pakistani army, which had a stake in the Taliban: here lay the clash of interest and probable cause for the "melting away" across the border to Pakistan.

Phase two of OEF confronted the coalition with a drastically altered

---

[9] Lieutenant General David W. Barno, 'Fighting the Other War – Counter Insurgency Strategy in Afghanistan 2003- 2005', Military Review- September-October 2007.

operational setting with a diluted and dispersed Taliban forced to use the population due to their earlier disintegration. This was the actual COIN phase, after the swift conventional first phase. The destruction of the conventional structure of the Taliban did not achieve the goal of denial of sanctuary to Al-Qaida and its associates. The large and disproportionate build up of forces that were the source of earlier victories now inhibited the successful conduct of operations. The primary reliance on attrition also alienated the very target of operations – the Afghan people. The Taliban dispersed after phase one, and on the contrary the coalition began a build up and became larger and concentrated leading to protracted chains of command with resultant delays in tactical application of force.

The singular reliance on use of technology to gather intelligence produced limited results as compared to human intelligence, even while the Taliban had an advantage by being dispersed within the population. The limitations of standard communication equipment and air support in the mountains were another operational learning that led to modification and innovation during operations. The deployment of Provincial Reconstruction Teams (PRTs) had limited success in the early days and faced opposition from aid agencies and NGOs working in the areas as it became difficult to differentiate between military operations and aid work thus inviting insurgent attacks on aid workers. The Taliban has avoided seeking contact and only chose contact on its own terms and in areas of choosing with dispersed combat and a networked organizational structure.

Pakistan Army and the War on Terror

The attacks of 9/11 caused Pakistan – which had officially recognized the Taliban- to quickly shift sides to supporting the US. Operations were initially undertaken by the FC along with regular army formations sent to the region and border-sealing operations were started. The army conducted operations from 2001 to 2010 in varying scales and has had mixed results in that they suffered casualties to ambushes and some soldiers surrendered.

Operations initially were more by inducting troops into tribal areas to dominate the area by sheer presence but the army suffered a series of losses and authorities signed deals with local militant leaders, which left militant groups in control. Control of operations was left to the Governor of FATA and the local superior military corps commander. Operation Sherdil (Lion Heart) in Bajaur in 2007 and Operation Rah-e- Haq (The True Path) in Malakand and Swat in 2008 were innovative in terms of learning COIN on the fly and gave the Pakistan Army initial learning and also led to some extreme application of principles when whole swathes of area were evacuated and cleared by reducing militant villages to rubble. The situation in FATA and erstwhile North West Frontier Province (NWFP) being under Taliban control after the army moved back into camps became unacceptable to the people of Pakistan. With the popular backing of the public, the army conducted Operation Rah-e-Rast (The Correct Path) in Swat with 52,000 troops and two wings of FC supported by special forces.[10]

The Pakistan army, with control primarily under the 11 Corps, is presently engaged in COIN operations in FATA and Khyber Pakhtunkhwa. The force with up to three divisions and police paramilitary and intelligence services are involved in operations along the Afghan border. The Frontier Corps, with a strength of 80,000, is now conducting the bulk of the fighting and the Special Services Group (SSG) – Pakistan's special forces – are performing search and destroy missions against Al Qaida and other high value targets. The use of special forces in an analogous method like the US of enemy-centric COIN, along with targeting of Taliban by drones, does clash with the people-centric attempts by the army and civil authorities in a renewed integrated deradicalization and disarmament programme. Pakistan also faces the impact of the scaling down of jihad for Kashmir ordered by President Pervez Musharraf in 2002, which has led to the redistribution of the militants into domestic terror networks that now also threaten Pakistan domestically.

Innovation: Paramilitary Forces

In order to correct the entrenched bias of conventional army structures, both in terms of doctrine and operational traditions, South Asia has witnessed the emergence of several organizational innovations in COIN, notably the creation

---

[10] Shuja Nawaz, 'Learning by Doing-The Pakistan Army's Experience with Counterinsurgency', Atlantic Council, February 2011, p 9-12.

of specialized paramilitary or proto-military forces with the specific function of dealing with domestic threats, including insurgencies. Three cases stand out.

India: Rashtriya Rifles

The deployment in the vast regions of J&K required additional troops and the army increased the raising of its fledgling counterinsurgency force called the Rashtriya Rifles (RR). *Rashtriya* means "national" and conveyed the sense of a force created to bind the nation. The force was initially inducted in to operations in Punjab during the period of the Sikh militancy in the 1980s. The force comprised of soldiers from all arms and services and was trained and specially equipped to counter insurgencies. Battalions are organized to be able to operate independently or under intermediate coordinating headquartersand have a mix of weapons specially found to be effective and versatile for fighting in built up areas and close quarter engagements. The sub units again are self sufficient and deploy in a grid to gain domination of the AOR.

The original purpose of creating a new paramilitary force was to relieve the army of its counterinsurgency burden to enable it to concentrate on the more conventional border protection tasks. The Indian paramilitary forces are much larger than the army and are large police-based, not trained or armed well enough to tackle insurgencies. When it was finally established, the RR became a completely army-based force once formal approval was granted in 1990. The 60 plus battalions of the RR have marginally offset the army's manpower commitment to counterinsurgency.[11] These battalions which were initially deployed to counter the insurgency in Punjab were effective due to their training, small logistical needs and area specific intelligence grids.

In Kashmir the RR battalions by virtue of being permanently committed to an affected area of insurgency in an effective counter insurgency grid have over the years provided valuable assistance in dominating the area and

---

[11] Rajesh Rajagopalan, 'Insurgency and counterinsurgency', http://www.indiaseminar.com/2009/599.htm.

executing operations to supplement the COIN efforts of the army. The battalions have established themselves with a sound intelligence network and are the main stay of implementing the civic action programmes in the battle to win hearts and minds.

Pakistan: Frontier Corps

In 2001, the Frontier Corps (FC) was deployed in the FATA region. The force was raised as a paramilitary force to be officered and staffed by the army. The force was organized along tribal groupings and based in the local tribal areas. The FC was poorly trained and inadequately equipped with antiquated weapons. The incentive to train and develop tactical acumen did not exist as the force conducted mainly policing and law and order duties and which was seen as lesser in status to the regular army in Pakistan. The tribal militias in the area had connections with their Afghan relatives and provided shelter and hospitality as per local customs to them when the invasion of Afghanistan drove them and the Taliban and Al-Qaida cadres into the border areas. The FC at this stage had no COIN capability and was not of much help to the army when it rolled in to the area. The FC were by some accounts entrusted with the task of facilitating the cross border movement of the Taliban into safe tribal areas of Pakistan during the 1980s and took time to adjust to the reversal of its role to that of a border sealing force.

The slow rejuvenation of the FC involved measures to improve service conditions, send in and promote officers, and equip the force with requisite weapons for the task. In 2007, the FC conducted operations in the Bajaur Agency for nearly eight months and regained some local tribal support. US assistance to the improved FC included training and basic equipment. Under a strong military leadership the FC in 2010 is credited with engaging the insurgents in the five agenciesof Mohmand, Orakzai, Kurram, Bajaur and Khyber.[12]

The Afghan National Army

In 2009 the reported strength of the Afghan National Army (ANA) was

---

[12] Shuja Nawaz, 'Learning by Doing-The Pakistan Army's Experience with Counterinsurgency', Atlantic Council, February 2011, p- 13.

80,000 and it is organized into five corps. Recruitment of the force with a balanced ethnic profile was initially a challenge as the Taliban paid locals more than the ISAF for service in their ranks. The gradual cohesion building within an ethnically diverse force and their training for combat roles is being achieved under the USFOR-A. The training with embedded training teams advising in four vital fields of communications, intelligence, fire support and infantry and logistic support is focused towards developing a soldier and NCO base. Equipping the ANA remains a concern and retention of equipment and accountability remain a challenge. The ANA is increasingly taking on a larger role in the conduct of operations with assistance from the US and allies in Afghanistan. The deputy commander of US forces in Afghanistan has cited a positive instance of active and increased participation of the ANA in areas of Helmand where a deployment of two battalions of marines has been reduced to only one company deployed as the ability of the Afghan security forces to provide the same level of security has improved.

Support: Employing Air Power and Technology

A notable feature of the Indian approach to COIN is that air power has not been used to strike at militants. This seemingly unremarkable facet of the strategy seems to stand out in contrast to the almost standard and integral element used by the United States in Afghanistan and by Pakistan in their frontier COIN campaigns. US forces rely intensively on the use of air strikes and the now ubiquitous drone strikes in operations against the Taliban, though with varied degrees of success and sometimes resulting in collateral damage that also damages the relationship with the Afghan population and the increasingly vocal government in Kabul.

In contrast, Indian COIN campaigns have been more calibrated, with an almost absolute restriction on use of heavy firepower such as artillery and air strikes. The ultimate aim of creating space for political negotiations and reconciliation dictate the elimination of any political obstacles such application of force could potentially cause. India's reluctance regarding the use of excessive force stems from the early Naga insurgency, when Prime Minister Jawaharlal Nehru denied the army's request to call in airpower support. The Indian Air Force has only been used in a support role for troop and logistic transportation and has not been eager to be involved in active COIN in the same logic of restraint that both the army has adopted.

There have been instances in COIN in India, most recently in the case of the *Naxalite* insurgency, when popular opinion has actively called for this restraint, which often translated into asking the army to fight with one hand tied to its back. However, the army has overall accepted the political limits imposed on its operational alternatives.

The US, on the other hand, is faced with the reliance on technology for reasons of force protection, avoidance of casualties to ground troops by minimizing direct contact and to make up for a shortage of manpower on the ground. Compensation for manpower and local tactical intelligence by technology such as space-based reconnaissance, communications and air power, paradoxically further decreases the "fighting" element of the force and diverts manpower from ground operations. Manpower is thus consumed in large maintenance and logistic detachments for keeping the helicopters, drones and other equipments in action. The local enemy thus fights with minimal technology and abundant local tactical intelligence, which forces US troops to face them with minimal intelligence and excessive reliance on technology to compensate for it, which, in turn, ironically reduces the size of combat contingents. In addition to the popular outrage against technical errors in targeting of innocents, and collateral damage in operations, the use of standoff weapons has tended to alienate the public from the military and make winning the hearts and minds so much more difficult.

Politics: The extra-military dimensions

India

In India, law and order is a "state" subject and is thus the responsibility of state governments. Their resources cater adequately for the normal crime and enforcement duties but fall short when faced with militant activities that challenge the state machinery. The central government assists the states in such cases and has paramilitary forces and counterterrorism forces, which are deployed in a graduated response. The success of COIN in democracies is demonstrated amply in the various instances in the Indian context where the democratic government has had political and popular support in its COIN efforts. The long term deployments of the armed forces in COIN is possible due to this consistent government policy emanating from this support which provides for the people to have numerous channels of communication and to voice their opinions.

Experience has shown that the police forces do not have the capacity to deal with insurgencies due to inexperienced combat leadership in insurgency and lack of weapons and equipment. The proxy natures of conflicts in Kashmir and the Northeast, the use of sophisticated weapons and equipment by the militants and the sheer violence unleashed have necessitated the deployment of the army in large numbers. The army is normally assisted by state forces to combat insurgencies and the police, and paramilitary forces come under command of the army during operations. For example, the task of organizing a coordinating the political and military campaign by the army and intelligence agencies to support the COIN grid in Kashmir was crucial to obviate the effects of stove piping. The Kashmir Monitoring Group focused on strategy and policy at the national level to be followed in Kashmir and has had mixed results. The Unified Headquarters, meant to coordinate political and military efforts, were established in J&K based on the Northeastern experience to synergize operations. The learning curve in this undertaking was long and sometimes disjointed due to lack of understanding of the purpose of the instituted coordination mechanism.

The political – military chord has at times faced tests when politicians have felt that the army operated without political sensitivity. The army tends to hold the political and bureaucratic class responsible for the shortsighted politics and poor governance that give rise to discord and violence leading up to insurgencies. On the other hand, the government has been consistent through most of the insurgencies with a primarily political approach towards resolving insurgency and rebellions. The use of the military is limited and always in a supportive role, although the use has been frequent and in large numbers. An inherent understanding however, has prevailed in the political and military leadership that the solutions to the disputes were political in nature, with restoration of normalcy from violence as the primary military role. The state has been willing to engage in political dialogue towards a resolution of the local demands, often even leading to creation of new states within the federal structure. A fairly large number of rebels have been accommodatedand become regional political leaders. Some of the salient political parameters guiding Indian COIN operations are:

- The integrity of the union is first and foremost and no breakup is acceptable.

- An anti-terror legislation and suitable laws to protect security forces is vital to the COIN effort.

- Political interests and criminal-political nexus are a force to reckon with.

- Control violence by joint COIN operations by the army, paramilitary and police.

- Intelligence of actionable nature is vital for surgical operations against militants.

- Respect for the religious and tribal sentiments of the local population and suitable psychological operations in advance of any intrusive operations to reduce alienation of the population.

Ideally, the regimentally motivated soldier prepared for conventional battle will have to be trained to carry out extremely delicate tasks with severe tactical restraint and light of these COIN imperatives above. Freedom to junior leaders is balanced against a conscious effort to curb the tendency to have too many tactical engagements as it meets the militant strategy of having a "sea of conflict".

The need is for calculated and deft tactical, psychological and political level of sophistication in daily operations such as ambushes, searches and interrogation of hostiles, civilians and identified over- ground supporters of the militants. For example, it is the political and human dimensions of unconventional warfare that has required a different approach in Kashmir from that in the Northeastern states. The main effort has been the unification of all efforts under a unified command structure comprising the political, military,police and moderates parties.The security forces after stabilizing the situation provide the secure environment for the politicalauthorities to provide governance.

The Politics of the Afghan War in America

President Obama's commitment to the war in Afghanistan is unquestionable and demonstrated by his tripling the strength of combat forces.The current strategy in Afghanistan is to enable the Afghan government to prevent the territory from being used as a safe haven for terrorists. It is perceived that a reengineering of Afghanistan is being attempted with an impressive infrastructure construction effort. However, the expectation of the US to settle for the main aim of prevention of terror is probably more pragmatic. The establishment of a permanent military base in Afghanistan to keep a check on the insurgency and to bring stability to Afghanistan is not a declared objective and the other projects being attempted within the COIN effort are in support of the main objective.

To avoid the risk of continued US commitment, the political acceptability of a negotiated settlement in Afghanistan is a factor to be considered. Though moves towards negotiations with the "moderates"are being attempted through the Afghan government of Hamid Karzai, its credibility will only be established when America seeks consensus *within* the country. To achieve a political consensus for a negotiated settlement at home is a major political step that the Administration will need to take in terms of giving the idea acceptability. The complex Afghan political structure and its traditional tribal loyalties and other complexities indicate that there has to be a settlement that may not be fully democratic in the way the Western world often wishes for. That such an arrangement may probably work in Afghanistan is not a certainty given the propensity of tribal affiliations to secure their parochial interest above that of the country. The effort to reach a loose political settlement by negotiating with the tribes is pragmatic and can be achieved by US influence on the outcome and is also possible, at least now that the surge has brought factions closer to negotiations. The clear focus on employment of the military as a tool to further political settlements and thereby usher stability and peace demonstrates the strong link between the political authority and the military. The surge will likely lead to the creation a durable political order by use of military strategy to deal with the primary US concern of denial of sanctuary to transnational threats.

On the other hand, the "civilian surge" in the wake of the military one has not materialized as anticipated. This undermines the Afghan government's ability to take control of the situation and may lead to extension of America's presence, which can cause drop in political support at home. The civilian surge was launched as part of an increased US focus on building government and economic institutions at the provincial level.The present governance being provided by civil-military teams was to be dismantled in 80 priority districts but security concerns have restricted the movement of civilian advisors to districts away from Kabul. Delays have adversely affected the District Delivery Programme, created to evaluate and staff local branches of government ministries. This delay in improving local governments in districts which the Taliban has targeted could impact the envisaged withdrawal of combat troops. Shortage of funds to those districts that have been evaluated has further exacerbated the existing shortage of capable civilian experts who can mentor Afghans in the field on basic civic tasks.

Civilian Casualties are one of the major causes for political discomfort. A report from the U.N.'s Assistance Mission in Afghanistan (UNAMA) attributed a rise in number of Afghan civilian deaths to insurgent actions such as IEDs and even assassination, and a decrease in deaths due to less collateral damage from ISAF actions.[13] Despite the fact that insurgents are responsible for an increase in killings, civilian casualties from coalition operations are a major source of strain in the already difficult relationship between President Hamid Karzai's government and the United States, and they generate widespread outrage among the population. The political dimensions of COIN seem to show, at least in this case, the complex relationship between the military, local government and the governments of foreign countries involved in restoration efforts.

Support of NATO partners is another consideration that vexes planners and decision makers in Washington. The US feels that the partners are more focused on relocation and withdrawal of troops rather than on what needs to be done for the reconstruction and rebuilding of Afghanistan. The transition to ANA from the ISAF is a matter of coordination between nations and the Afghan government and disjointed withdrawals have potential to cede security gains made to individual national politics of partner countries.

Pakistan's political inaction

Political involvement in Pakistan has been either nonexistent or reluctant at

---

[13] Ernesto Londono, 'U.N. alarmed by surge in civilian casualties in Afghanistan', Washington Post, 9 March 2011.

best;not surprising considering that the military has ruled the country for more than fifty years. The lack of political interest in FATA stems from the days of British rule and creation of a buffer zone. The entire region was left to operate under tribal laws and no political party operated there. The area was often governed remotely by civil servants or political agents. The occasional unrest by the tribes against the civil government were met with government handouts to tribal leaders and led to rampant corruption and nepotism.

The sudden influx of the army into the area after 2001 saw the tribal leaders and local civil representatives relegated to the background of the operations in the areas. The army which was used to being in control did not consult and fortify itself with knowledge to leverage local affiliations and underestimated the ability of the tribal militia to fight on home turf. The resulting reverses suffered by the army led to it signing deals with local militants without consulting tribal elders and civil administrators. This further reduced the sway of these representatives of civil rule. This absence of a total coordinated approach with involvement of the local population and civil administration was clearly perceptible and led to ineffective outcomes of early COIN operations by the army in Malakand, Swat and North Waziristan upto as late as 2008.

The political configuration of governance of FATA and the border areas was radically altered by Al Qaida and the Taliban. They eliminated the local elected leaders (*maliks*) and replaced the consultative body (*jirga*) with councils (*shura*) that had no appeal process and garnered local support in the name of a holy war against foreigners. A slow regaining of the faith of local leaders and tribal elders was initiated during the Bajaur operations by the military. The army tried to build national consensus towards COIN but collaboration between the political class, and more recently the civil government, and the military was inadequate despite a perceptible connection between COIN and counterterrorism operations. The spate of terror attacks in Pakistan in 2009 reflected the lack of serious civil – military interaction so badly needed to promulgate new laws for protection of the population. The Taliban's declaration of the constitution of the country as un-Islamic and its insistence on providing shelter to the Al Qaida leadership has served as a catalyst for a political consensus building process that has since then brought religious moderates on board for further COIN efforts.

Reconstruction: Winning Hearts and Minds

Indian Army's Operation *Sadhbhavana*

Operation Sadhbhavana ("goodwill") was initiated in 1998 in Jammu and Kashmir, when the army launched its civic action programme. This initiative illustrates how the Indian Army has innovated from its conventional war fighting bias to a more nuanced approach which is people–centric. The fundamental principles of use of minimum force and the people as a centre of gravity have evolved into the conduct of welfare-oriented army projects. Guided by the objectives to win hearts and minds, the army focused on three major activities: elections, revival of tourism and countering of subversive propaganda. The army, on its watch has overseen the conduct of two elections and provided a stable and safe atmosphere conducive to development. It was in the third action of countering militant propaganda that the projects to integrate the population were initiated by the army and were immensely well received. The main focus of such actions is "to help people to help themselves". The initiative, was conceptualized as one of the lines of operation as part of the overall counterinsurgency strategy. It was aimed at achieving the two goals of wresting the initiative from the terrorists and to reintegrate the population into the national mainstream.

A set of guiding principles dictates the selection and execution of projects under Sadhbavana. These are:

- Projects must be based on popular demand to have a high impact.
- Planning must be centralised and execution decentralised.
- Projects must be iniated mainly at the village level.
- Projects must be aimed at self empowerment of people.
- Projects must be sustainable.

- Integration of civic activities with state administration and community development plans.

The role of the government in the reestablishment of governance is seen asthe most difficult one. Ideally, the civilian local administration and the state government should initiate activities in the cleared areas under the watch of the security forces.There is a perceptible reluctance of government workers to return to disturbed areas where militant actions and harassment, extortion by the local *mafia* on trucks and other means of transportation are serious deterrents. This, however, is sometimes used by the administration as an excuse to cover up for lack of institutional capacity of the state machinery and to prolong employment of the military. This problem is usually solved by urging the Army to take on the task of reconstruction and rehabilitation. The simplicity of the solution and the political expediency in exercising of the chain of command of the Unified HQ is so tempting and usually the preferred choice of the civil administration. Such extension of the army from basic Sadhbhavna tasks to full-fledged reconstruction activities along with security to the movement of reconstruction material leads to a dilution of the pure military role of the army and morphs into an onerous responsibility for the local unit or formation commander.

The Indian Army is now emphasizing the theme "My heart is my weapon". 2011 has been declared as the year of education, health and economic progress, objectives that are forwarded as the hallmarks of a return to normalcy. While it may be premature to point towards tangible successes, the *Awam* (people) – *Jawan* (soldier) cooperation has been given a positive momentum by the army with its latest campaign of *AwamaurJawan – AmanhaiMuqam* ("people and the soldier strive for peace together"). Measures include a revision of convoy size and timings, with an aim to have minimum disturbance to the civilian population. At the same time, a whole new approach to being effective and dominating the disturbed areas without displaying aggressive intent is being attempted with education on more nuanced behaviour towards women, the elderly, children and the normal civilian. The change of attitude is what is most important to achieve to win the battle of "hearts and minds". The sudden transition to an attitude in COIN is one of the aims of the various counterinsurgency schools that orient newly inducted battalions and turned-over troops to nuances of the "velvet glove on the iron fist".

Afghanistan and the Success of the PRTs

The effort put into"The three Rs" (Regain-Rebuild-Resolve) by PRTs in Afghanistan is now looked upon as a key to the ISAF strategy. The 26 PRTs are involved in extending the central government's authority throughout the country by providing area security and supporting reconstruction and development activities of all agencies. Some of the teams consist of military and civilian members from a single ISAF country and some are multinational. A wide variety of projects such as rebuilding of schools, irrigation schemes with pipelines, wells and reservoirs are being undertaken alongside reconstruction of infrastructure like bridges and roads and medical attention to the locals.

The money and strength of the US is driving a hearts and minds campaign in the show piece town of Marja in Helmand province of Afghanistan. The programme of development of roads, street lighting and goodies such as grants and enrollment of able-bodied men into defence militias is at work in the district.The setting up of Interim Security for Critical Infrastructure (ISCI) teams by the US army formed of local fighters from the region as a militia is both a means of security as it is of empowerment and thus winning the hearts of the locals by the largesse of cash and goodies. This build up of local forces is not going down well with the government in Kabul, which fears a slippage into warlordism. The lavish effort to create local governance and security is likely to face the wrath of the Taliban in the summer when the fighting is expected to erupt.

The creation of an organization from within the locals is seen by the US as a turnabout and a step towards establishment of some sort of formal governance by the locals – an essential prerequisite for the withdrawal of US forces eventually. The fear of retribution by the Taliban is slowly eroding away and more volunteers are forthcoming in this effort. The conduct of elections in September 2010 is considered as the turning point by many when the Afghan army and police forces put together a plan to defend the polling stations. The hope of putting up more schools and electricity also drives the local support, which sees cooperation with the Marines as mutually beneficial. The next step is forming a bond with the government of the country.

Pakistan Army: Hold and Build

The Swat operations have brought a realization to the Pakistan military that population support and their protection and development are primary to achieve the de-radicalization of the youth and locals. As soon as operations to clear the Taliban reached culmination the operation to win the populations support commenced. The first steps were the relocation of the locals and rebuilding and reconstruction by army teams without reliance on the provincial government or the almost defunct bureaucracy. Projects that rebuilt or created schools, restored damaged mosques, conducted forestation and repair to private homes damaged in the army operations have been successfully received. Restoration of infrastructure such as roads and bridges very critical for communication and movement of the population have had a positive impact as well as new medical camps and supplies. The training of local youth for employment opportunities has been done in an attempt to win back the youth. The army has also been involved in training of community police and the enrollment of police officers in Malakand and Swat.

In the operations in Bajaur in 2008, the first attempts to garner local support albeit for operational gains were attempted. The local tribal leaders and tribal militias were co-opted to divide the pro-Taliban and pro-government elements. The strategy was used to further success in 2009, in Swat, when the population protection approach was adopted by patrolling and supporting local militias to identify radical Taliban who refused to reconcile. The economic condition of the locals was assessed to be reliant on tourism that was nonexistentsince the war. With more than half the population between the ages of 18 and 24, the only and probably best paymaster was the Taliban that paid youth to kill the foreigners – and the Pakistani army was considered foreign to this areas. This led to assessments of the local projects to develop the area's infrastructure and provide jobs to locals at the same time. The army has spent almost 515 million rupees (approximately US$ 12 million) in such efforts.[14]

---

[14] Ernesto Londono, 'U.N. alarmed by surge in civilian casualties in Afghanistan', Washington Post, 9 March 2011.

Reconciliation: Peace as a Process

J&K: The need for Reconciliation

The present situation in J&K is one in which insurgency related violence and terror has noticed a steady drop since it first began two decades ago. The history of the rise of militancy can be traced to the 90s when the army was deployed to curb the rising violence in the state. By the mid-nineties the army had seized the initiative from the militants and established a COIN grid in tiers within the state to both check infiltration across the LOC and also to ensure dominance in the rest of the state. A second cycle of rise in militancy was noticed after the Kargil invasion by Pakistan and the military operations thereafter to evict the intruders. The COIN grid was disrupted and militants took advantage by upping the ante to *fedeyeen* attacks. It took upto 2003 for the army to regain dominance and in 2003 a ceasefire was declared which allowed the completion of the border fence project along the line of the LOC. The effective border management posture and the establishment of two tiers of COIN grid by the army has drastically brought down militancy and violence to a state of near normalcy. The army has enabled conduct of two elections in which the voter turnout was a stunning revelation of the population's desire for peace and the denouncement of terror and violence. Over the present decade a sound political strategy of keeping a humane approach to the concerns of the population has resulted in a juncture where the state government has functioned to provide governance and development.

A growing recognition in India that the control of insurgency is not an event but rather a process has produced a policy which is an amalgam of use of the military, respect for human rights of the population and effective governance by an elected government. The government of India has announced an eight point plan to go about the process of resolving tensions that erupted in late 2010. The plan envisages the appointment of a interlocutor for negotiations between various groups and release of a majority of demonstrators especially students. The imposing military presence and visible bunkers of security personnel in the cities and towns are to be redeployed in an effort to achieve a semblance of normalcy. The list of government declared disturbed areas is being reviewed with a view to reduce the influence of the

AFSPA – a long standing demand of the protestors. The measures aim at assuaging the prevalent feelings of a heavy handed COIN strategy applied by the central government. A combination of giving a voice to the population and control of violence by the security forces is expected to give peace a chance in the embattled state.

Outlook in Afghanistan and Pakistan

The summer of 2011 in Afghanistan presents a changed landscape both to the insurgents and the ISAF. A concerted campaign of elimination of the local support bases of the Taliban has put into place local bodies of governance and defence comprised of Afghan officials and tribal defence groups. The operations by special forces and local contingents to eliminate supporters of the Taliban have reduced effective areas where the Taliban returning in the summer can expect sustenance. The level of violence has usually dipped in the winters but a Taliban resurgence in the spring is likely to be aimed at taking back former strongholds, particularly the areas where the insurgents raised money through opium trafficking. It is expected that the Taliban will mount a spring campaign to regain ground lost to US troops last year and use suicide bombing teams to strike at those associated with the Afghan government or coalition forces. In the erstwhile insurgent strongholds in the south and east, it is believed that the operations in the past have now made troops better positioned than they were last year to fend off the insurgency, now that they have 70,000 new Afghan forces and have seized control of some Taliban sanctuaries.

Safe havens in Pakistan protect the Taliban leadership and allow its ranks to regenerate and the return by the Taliban has been stronger after the winter rest with greater reach and newer tactics. The expected tactic of choice this time is assassination of local leaders and attacking soft targets. The precursor of this strategy can be seen in the recent suicide bombings targeting public places, banks and hotels. Rampant government corruption and frustration of the people with the presence of foreign forces could undermine public support. There is a growing realization amongst the military leadership in Afghanistan that the insurgency can never be totally eliminated. The need for building strong support for the Afghan people to increase their participation in their own governance has set a goal to provide a level of security that would allow Afghans to resume their normal lives.

While it is in Afghanistan where the US and the coalition are engaged in COIN, it is however more important for a stable South Asia that COIN succeeds in Pakistan. COIN in Pakistan is handicapped and military successes are wasted by the absence of a strong civil government. There are parties in Pakistan who look upon US financial and military support in the region as a handy leverage to exert in return for Pakistan's commitment to COIN. The anti-India position of Pakistan manifests itself in the equation in Afghanistan, a country which Pakistan sees as providing strategic depth to its interests. Despite Pakistan's COIN campaign against the Taliban and Al-Qaida within the country it needs to reorient its strategic calculus. The US effort in Afghanistan toward the establishment of a stable Afghan government that can neutralize the terror groups presently backed from across the border in Pakistan can facilitate that reorientation.

The US success in Afghanistan is likely to be a turning point in the present conundrum of Pakistan and terrorism. As of now, the growing instability in Pakistan, its connections to terror groups through the ISI and the military and existence of safe havens are challenges acknowledged by US Pentagon planners and policy makers alike. The terrorists groups operating from Pakistan are a cause of serious concern. ISAF forces can counter them in Afghanistan; but to handle them in Pakistan, especially after the limitations that Islamabad imposes on operations on Pakistani soil, the US will have to rely on Pakistan. The US will need to build an effective partnership that advances both US and Pakistani interests, while also demonstrating that it remains a strong supporter of their security and prosperity over the longterm – a fear not without precedent in Pakistan. It is only when the denial of safe havens to terror groups is made a central aligning factor of US and Pakistani relations that a long term relationship can emerge and bring tranquility to the region.

Conclusion: Lessons from South Asia

The learning curve is almost invariably flat when armies first get involved in COIN operations. The proverbial "reinventing the wheel" seems to occur with unfailing regularity- one COIN experience may bring lessons to the fore, but these hard-won lessons are then abandoned and have to be relearned subsequently. As exemplified in the case of South Asia, militaries of most countries tend to develop a conventional bias based on their organization and evolution, which obfuscates lessons learnt from dealing with earlier insurgencies. This lack of "COIN memory" is a major obstacle, especially in a region so diverse as South Asia, in which insurgencies have proliferated. Training and preparation for COIN at all levels will help coordinate an integrated approach. But even more urgent is the institutionalization of the "lessons learned" at the political, military and administrative levels of COIN. What follows are some of the main imperatives to a successful COIN strategy, at least as reflected in the common thread of the three approaches analyzed in this paper.

First, the overall benefits of integrating political and military strategies to gain maximum impact amplifies the need for involvement of local political governments to allow COIN to gain legitimacy in the eyes of the population. As a corollary, to give credit to the local government for success in initiatives reduces the militants' seditious propaganda effect. In Afghanistan, as in Pakistan and India, the essential emergence of a strongcivilian government will erode the fear of the insurgents and deny them sanctuary. The Indian experience is particularly relevant, in that it focuses on the restoration of the credibility of local administration and on winning over the support of the population. The development of under-governed and remote areas is thus the turning point in COIN and it is this – not superior manpower and technology –that defeats insurgents.

Second, democracies do seem able to guarantee better popular support in a tough war. The support the Indian Government gets due to its political legitimacy, despite serious mishandling in some instances, is long standing proof of this. In Pakistan, the COIN campaigns during the autocratic military rule of Musharraf did not get as much backing of the people and even by some sections of the army. On the other hand the democratic government of Asif Ali Zardariearned the wholehearted backing of the people duringthe 2009 operations in Swat and Malakand. The US effort to bestow credit on Hamid Karzai forincreasedgovernance and its handing over of control to the Afghan Army and Police also relies on the primacy of democratic government.

Third, COIN in a foreign country is far more difficult and drains resources exponentially as compared to operations *within* the borders of the nation. The wide political support for the army within its own country when it is engaged in COIN makes the effort easier in terms of achieving restoration and governance.The Indian experience of not losing in COIN within its boundaries, contrasting with its negative experience abroad in Sri Lanka, proves this. In contrast, the US, and also to an extent Pakistan at the beginning of its campaign, were in conditions more likely to be seen as occupation forces and against the will of people of differing ethnic, political and cultural backgrounds. Here lies the relevance of building local forces by training, developing interoperability and ultimately transferring responsibilities to them.

Fourth, intelligence is paramount in COIN operations as it helps avoid wasteful deployment of scarce resources and destroys the insurgent's local tactical advantage. At the strategic level the awareness of alliances and linkages between socially networked insurgent and terror groups allows for preemption in planning operations and to achieve disintegration amongst insurgent groups to benefit towards a negotiated settlement.

Fifth, given that insurgents and separatists rely primarily on external sources and actors for strength, resources, training and intelligence, COIN needs to have an enlarged scope of action that transcends territorial borders. The case of Pakistan's influence in Punjab in India, Chinese support to the insurgencies in the Northeastern states of India, the Taliban in FATA and Afghanistan, are examples of external players' influence in already complex situations. Any successful COIN campaign has to cut off such external support.

Sixth, the creation of specialist COIN forces does help in keeping COIN knowledge current and relevant to new operational contexts, however different. The Rashtriya Rifles in India have been effectively deployed in COIN in Kashmir for nearly two decades and, despite its internal rotation of troops, retention of institutional knowledge has beentremendous. The Pakistani experience with the FC was initially poor but over constant engagement the FC is now in the forefront of operations. The US rotation every nine months makes relearning COIN much more challenging to the newly arrived troops.

In conclusion, the comparison of COIN in South Asia suggests that devising aone-solution-fits-all-problems approach has not worked in the three cases. The case of Iraq for the US, the differences between Kashmir and the Northeastern insurgencies in India, and the contingent and deal-oriented COIN in Pakistan, all gave rise to important lessons learnt at extremely high costs over repeated deployment. The governments involved have also applied an integrated approach in fits and starts thus taking a"sometimes-on, sometimes-off" perspective that confused and diverted the COIN effort at the military level. The conventional armies have reconciled to the political nature of COIN and increased their political flexibility in seeking solutions to tackle insurgency. The Indian success to defeat insurgencies by conduct of elections and transfer of governance to local actors is being confirmedby the US persistence in dealing with the democratic government in Afghanistan in order to reconstruct and restore civilian control over the country.

Contributors

Shri EN Rammohan, IPS (Retd). Shri EN Rammohan is 1965 Batch Assam Cadre, Indian Police Service officer. He retired from service as Director General of the Border Security Force in November 2000. After retirement, he has had a tenure as Advisor to the Governor of Manipur.

He has extensive experience of combating insurgency. He has personal knowledge of the Northeast and has very close association with the people and with the Police Forces in the Northeast. He has served in the state of Jammu and Kashmir as well as in the Northeast.

Brigadier Amrit Pal Singh. Brigadier Amrit Pal Singh is pursuing an Executive Masters degree in Intelligence Analysis at the University of Maryland. His wide-ranging 30-years long service in the Indian Army included responsibilities as a peacekeeper with the United Nations in Liberia and as a director in the Integrated Headquarters of the Ministry of Defence, New Delhi. He has been awarded two Masters degrees, one in Political Science from Osmania Univesity, Hyderabad, and another in Defence and Strategic Studies from The University of Madras, Chennai. He has published insights and comments in various defence and security journals.

Gp Capt AK Agarwal. GpCapt AK Agarwal is an alumini of the National Defence Academy Khadakwasla, Pune. He was commissioned into the Indian Air Force on 04 June 1982, as a pilot in the fighter stream. He has over 2400 hours of flying various aircraft. The officer is a Qualified Flying Instructor. He has undergone the Defence Services Staff Course and the Higher Defence Management Course at the College of Defence Management. Currently the officer is on study leave and is working as Senior Research Fellow at the USI.

www.ingramcontent.com/pod-product-compliance
Lightning Source LLC
Chambersburg PA
CBHW070810300326
41914CB00078B/1932/J